Lecture Notes in Computer Science

Vol. 296: R. Janßen (Ed.), Trends in Computer Algebra. Proceedings, 1987. V, 197 pages. 1988.

Vol. 297: E.N. Houstis, T.S. Papatheodorou, C.D. Polychronopoulos (Eds.), Supercomputing. Proceedings, 1987. X, 1093 pages. 1988.

Vol. 298: M. Main, A. Melton, M. Mislove, D. Schmidt (Eds.), Mathematical Foundations of Programming Language Semantics. Proceedings, 1987. VIII, 637 pages. 1988.

Vol. 299: M. Dauchet, M. Nivat (Eds.), CAAP '88. Proceedings, 1988. VI, 304 pages. 1988.

Vol. 300: H. Ganzinger (Ed.), ESOP '88. Proceedings, 1988. VI, 381 pages. 1988.

Vol. 301: J. Kittler (Ed.), Pattern Recognition. Proceedings, 1988. VII, 668 pages. 1988.

Vol. 302: D.M. Yellin, Attribute Grammar Inversion and Source-to-source Translation. VIII, 176 pages. 1988.

Vol. 303: J.W. Schmidt, S. Ceri, M. Missikoff (Eds.), Advances in Database Technology – EDBT '88. X, 620 pages. 1988.

Vol. 304: W.L. Price, D. Chaum (Eds.), Advances in Cryptology – EUROCRYPT '87. Proceedings, 1987. VII, 314 pages. 1988.

Vol. 305: J. Biskup, J. Demetrovics, J. Paredaens, B. Thalheim (Eds.), MFDBS 87. Proceedings, 1987. V, 247 pages. 1988.

Vol. 306: M. Boscarol, L. Carlucci Aiello, G. Levi (Eds.), Foundations of Logic and Functional Programming. Proceedings, 1986. V, 218 pages. 1988.

Vol. 307: Th. Beth, M. Clausen (Eds.), Applicable Algebra, Error-Correcting Codes, Combinatorics and Computer Algebra. Proceedings, 1986. VI, 215 pages. 1988.

Vol. 308: S. Kaplan, J.-P. Jouannaud (Eds.), Conditional Term Rewriting Systems. Proceedings, 1987. VI, 278 pages. 1988.

Vol. 309: J. Nehmer (Ed.), Experiences with Distributed Systems. Proceedings, 1987. VI, 292 pages. 1988.

Vol. 310: E. Lusk, R. Overbeek (Eds.), 9th International Conference on Automated Deduction. Proceedings, 1988. X, 775 pages. 1988.

Vol. 311: G. Cohen, P. Godlewski (Eds.), Coding Theory and Applications 1986. Proceedings, 1986. XIV, 196 pages. 1988.

Vol. 312: J. van Leeuwen (Ed.), Distributed Algorithms 1987. Proceedings, 1987. VII, 430 pages. 1988.

Vol. 313: B. Bouchon, L. Saitta, R.R. Yager (Eds.), Uncertainty and Intelligent Systems. IPMU '88. Proceedings, 1988. VIII, 408 pages. 1988.

Vol. 314: H. Göttler, H.J. Schneider (Eds.), Graph-Theoretic Concepts in Computer Science. Proceedings, 1987. VI, 254 pages. 1988.

Vol. 315: K. Furukawa, H. Tanaka, T. Fujisaki (Eds.), Logic Programming '87. Proceedings, 1987. VI, 327 pages. 1988.

Vol. 316: C. Choffrut (Ed.), Automata Networks. Proceedings, 1986. VII, 125 pages. 1988.

Vol. 317: T. Lepistö, A. Salomaa (Eds.), Automata, Languages and Programming. Proceedings, 1988. XI, 741 pages. 1988.

Vol. 318: R. Karlsson, A. Lingas (Eds.), SWAT 88. Proceedings, 1988. VI, 262 pages. 1988.

Vol. 319: J.H. Reif (Ed.), VLSI Algorithms and Architectures – AWOC 88. Proceedings, 1988. X, 476 pages. 1988.

Vol. 320: A. Blaser (Ed.), Natural Language at the Computer. Proceedings, 1988. III, 176 pages. 1988.

Vol. 321: J. Zwiers, Compositionality, Concurrency and Partial Correctness. VI, 272 pages. 1989.

Vol. 322: S. Gjessing, K. Nygaard (Eds.), ECOOP '88. European Conference on Object-Oriented Programming. Proceedings, 1988. VI, 410 pages. 1988.

Vol. 323: P. Deransart, M. Jourdan, B. Lorho, Attribute Grammars. IX, 232 pages. 1988.

Vol. 324: M.P. Chytil, L. Janiga, V. Koubek (Eds.), Mathematical Foundations of Computer Science 1988. Proceedings. IX, 562 pages. 1988.

Vol. 325: G. Brassard, Modern Cryptology. VI, 107 pages. 1988.

Vol. 326: M. Gyssens, J. Paredaens, D. Van Gucht (Eds.), ICDT '88. 2nd International Conference on Database Theory. Proceedings, 1988. VI, 409 pages. 1988.

Vol. 327: G.A. Ford (Ed.), Software Engineering Education. Proceedings, 1988. V, 207 pages. 1988.

Vol. 328: R. Bloomfield, L. Marshall, R. Jones (Eds.), VDM '88. VDM – The Way Ahead. Proceedings, 1988. IX, 499 pages. 1988.

Vol. 329: E. Börger, H. Kleine Büning, M.M. Richter (Eds.), CSL '87. 1st Workshop on Computer Science Logic. Proceedings, 1987. VI, 346 pages. 1988.

Vol. 330: C.G. Günther (Ed.), Advances in Cryptology – EUROCRYPT '88. Proceedings, 1988. XI, 473 pages. 1988.

Vol. 331: M. Joseph (Ed.), Formal Techniques in Real-Time and Fault-Tolerant Systems. Proceedings, 1988. VI, 229 pages. 1988.

Vol. 332: D. Sannella, A. Tarlecki (Eds.), Recent Trends in Data Type Specification. V, 259 pages. 1988.

Vol. 333: H. Noltemeier (Ed.), Computational Geometry and its Applications. Proceedings, 1988. VI, 252 pages. 1988.

Vol. 334: K.R. Dittrich (Ed.), Advances in Object-Oriented Database Systems. Proceedings, 1988. VII, 373 pages. 1988.

Vol. 335: F.A. Vogt (Ed.), CONCURRENCY 88. Proceedings, 1988. VI, 401 pages. 1988.

Vol. 336: B.R. Donald, Error Detection and Recovery in Robotics. XXIV, 314 pages. 1989.

Vol. 337: O. Günther, Efficient Structures for Geometric Data Management. XI, 135 pages. 1988.

Vol. 338: K.V. Nori, S. Kumar (Eds.), Foundations of Software Technology and Theoretical Computer Science. Proceedings, 1988. IX, 520 pages. 1988.

Vol. 339: M. Rafanelli, J.C. Klensin, P. Svensson (Eds.), Statistical and Scientific Database Management. Proceedings, 1988. IX, 454 pages. 1989.

Vol. 340: G. Rozenberg (Ed.), Advances in Petri Nets 1988. VI, 439 pages. 1988.

Vol. 341: S. Bittanti (Ed.), Software Reliability Modelling and Identification. VII, 209 pages. 1988.

Vol. 342: G. Wolf, T. Legendi, U. Schendel (Eds.), Parcella '88. Proceedings, 1988. 380 pages. 1989.

Vol. 343: J. Grabowski, P. Lescanne, W. Wechler (Eds.), Algebraic and Logic Programming. Proceedings, 1988. 278 pages. 1988.

Vol. 344: J. van Leeuwen, Graph-Theoretic Concepts in Computer Science. Proceedings, 1988. VII, 459 pages. 1989.

Vol. 345: R.T. Nossum (Ed.), Advanced Topics in Artificial Intelligence. VII, 233 pages. 1988 (Subseries LNAI).

Vol. 346: M. Reinfrank, J. de Kleer, M.L. Ginsberg, E. Sandewall (Eds.), Non-Monotonic Reasoning. Proceedings, 1988. XIV, 237 pages. 1989 (Subseries LNAI).

Vol. 347: K. Morik (Ed.), Knowledge Representation and Organization in Machine Learning. XV, 319 pages. 1989 (Subseries LNAI).

Vol. 348: P. Deransart, B. Lorho, J. Maluszyński (Eds.), Programming Languages Implementation and Logic Programming. Proceedings, 1988. VI, 299 pages. 1989.

Vol. 349: B. Monien, R. Cori (Eds.), STACS 89. Proceedings, 1989. VIII, 544 pages. 1989.

Vol. 350: A. Törn, A. Žilinskas, Global Optimization. X, 255 pages. 1989.

Vol. 351: J. Díaz, F. Orejas (Eds.), TAPSOFT '89. Volume 1. Proceedings, 1989. X, 383 pages. 1989.

Lecture Notes in Computer Science

Edited by G. Goos and J. Hartmanis

400

Rolf Klein

Concrete and Abstract
Voronoi Diagrams

Springer-Verlag

Berlin Heidelberg New York London Paris Tokyo Hong Kong

Author

Rolf Klein
Universität-Gesamthochschule-Essen, Fachbereich Mathematik
Praktische Informatik mit Schwerpunkt Softwareorientierte Informatik
Schützenbahn 70, D-4300 Essen 1, FRG

CR Subject Classification (1987): E.1, F.2.2, H.3.3, I.3.5

ISBN 3-540-52055-4 Springer-Verlag Berlin Heidelberg New York
ISBN 0-387-52055-4 Springer-Verlag New York Berlin Heidelberg

Printing and binding: Druckhaus Beltz, Hemsbach/Bergstr.
2145/3140-543210 – Printed on acid-free paper

Contents

Preface   1

Introduction   3

1   Voronoi diagrams in nice metrics   9
1.1   The Euclidean Voronoi diagram   9
1.2   Nice metrics   16

2   Abstract Voronoi diagrams   31
2.1   Definitions   32
2.2   Elementary properties   34
2.3   The neighborhoods of points in V(S)   36
2.4   Augmented curve systems   43
2.5   The shape of the Voronoi regions   46
2.6   The graph structure of abstract Voronoi diagrams   51
2.7   Characterizing Voronoi diagrams   52

3   Computing abstract Voronoi diagrams   63
3.1   Representing the Voronoi diagram   64
3.2   The divide-and-conquer approach   67
3.3   Bisecting chains   73
3.4   The non-degenerate case   77
3.4.1 Determining endpoints of chain segments   77
3.4.2 Finding the continuing segment   92
3.4.3 The complete algorithm   97
3.5   The degenerate case   99
3.5.1 Local separation of curves   101
3.5.2 Cross-points   109
3.5.3 The modified algorithm   112

4   Acyclic partitions   131

4.1   Supported d-circles 131
4.2   Simply-connected d-circles 140
4.3   The Moscow metric 147

Concluding Remarks   159

Bibliography   163

Preface

The Voronoi diagram is one of the most useful data structures in computational geometry, with applications in many areas of science. In this book, a unifying approach is proposed by introducing abstract Voronoi diagrams. These are not based on the notion of distance but rather on the concept of bisecting curves.

This book is a revised version of my Habilitationsschrift *On a generalization of planar Voronoi diagrams* that was accepted by the Faculty of Mathematics, University of Freiburg, FRG, in February 1989. I have included some recent developments, and have brought up to date the selection of open problems in the concluding remarks.

I want to thank the Institute of Computer Science, the Faculty of Mathematics, and the University of Freiburg, for their support. Special thanks to Christine Krause and Lihong Ma, who did an excellent job in LaTeXing the manuscript!

I am grateful to Walter Nef, Hartmut Noltemeier, Joachim Nitsche, Thomas Ottmann, Peter Widmayer, and John Wieacker, who gave their opinion on this work, and to the anonymous referees. Their interest, good will, and patience be thanked!

A great debt of gratitude I owe to Anne Brüggemann-Klein, Kurt Mehlhorn, and Derick Wood. Derick came up with the topic of proximity problems in cities and, thereby, gave rise to this work. He also joined in, during the last weeks of my stay with the Data Structuring Group in Waterloo in 1987. Kurt encouraged me to publish these Lecture Notes. His appreciation was as rewarding as the fact that he, together with Colm Ó'Dúnlaing and Stefan Meiser, continued the research begun in my thesis. Without Anne's support, this book would not be the same. The discussions with her helped me to clarify my thoughts, she cheered me up when I needed it, and—she drew the figures in this text. Thanks to all of you!

Essen, October 1989   Rolf Klein

Introduction

The goal of this book is to provide tools for the efficient computation of Voronoi diagrams in the plane.

In general, if a finite set S of objects p_i is given in a space M, computing the Voronoi diagram of S means to partition the space into regions, $R(p_i, S)$, in such a way that $R(p_i, S)$ contains all points of M that are closer to p_i than to any other object p_j in S. Clearly, this statement must be made precise: One has to define what kind of objects ("sites") are considered, and what the underlying distance measure in space M is. Furthermore, it must be specified what to do with those points of M that have more than one nearest neighbor in S.

Such partitions play an important role in various areas of science. The first who used them was Dirichlet [21], in a paper on the reduction of quadratic forms; his objects were the points of a lattice in the Euclidean plane (some authors [5] consider Descartes [19] the inventor of Voronoi diagrams. In fact, the vortices, space consists of in his view, form a partition much like Voronoi diagrams, but no explicit rule seems to be imposed on the extension of the regions). Though Voronoi's work [59,58] on quadratic forms appeared half a century later than Dirichlet's, the partitions in question have been called after him in computer science. Synonymous names are *Dirichlet tessellations* or *tilings*, *Wigner-Seitz cells*, and *Thiessen polygons*. Applications of the Voronoi diagram, besides those in mathematics and in computer science, are in archaeology, biology, crystallography, and physics; references can be found in [23], [5], and [7]. Lately, it was reinvented in art [48], as a "regents graphic".

The Voronoi diagram was introduced to computer science by Shamos and Hoey [56]. They studied the case of an object set, S, consisting of n points in the Euclidean plane (possibly irregularly placed), and presented an algorithm that allows the Voronoi diagram, $V(S)$, of S to be constructed in time proportional to $n \log n$, in the worst case; see Figure 1.2. This result provided solutions to a number of *proximity problems* that soon became of vital importance to the rapidly growing branch of computational geometry. For example, if S contains n elements then a *closest pair* in $S \times S$ can be read off the Voronoi diagram within a number of steps linear in n (see Section 1.1), which leads to an $O(n \log n)$ worst case solution to the closest pair problem. As compared to the naive approach that takes $\binom{n}{2}$ many steps, a result like this is not just an improvement: In practice, if $n \sim 10^6$ and if the constants hidden in the "big-O"notation are not extremely large, an $O(n \log n)$ algorithm can do within some minutes what would take the quadratic algorithm several months; this often marks the difference between the feasible and the impossible (see Column 7 in [9]). The algorithm presented in [56] is asymptotically worst case optimal, with respect to both time and space. Other optimal algorithms were introduced later [11,25].

As computational geometry developed, the concept of the Euclidean Voronoi diagram of a planar point set was generalized in different ways.

Alreadly in [56], the Euclidean k^{th}-*order Voronoi diagram* was introduced. Here with each subset T of S of size k the region

$$R(T, S) = \{z \in \Re^2; \forall t \in T \forall s \in S - T : |t - z| \leq |s - z|\}$$

is associated. At most $O(n^3)$ many regions of all orders k, $1 \leq k \leq n-1$, are non-empty; yet it is surprising that the collection of all k^{th}-order Voronoi diagrams can be computed in time $O(n^3)$ [24]. The kth-order Voronoi diagram can be used in solving *clustering problems* [28].

Point sets in *higher dimensional Euclidean space* were considered, and an interesting relation to the *convex hull* of a finite point set was revealed, see Section 1.1. Voronoi diagrams of objects such as *planar curve segments* [61] proved valuable in *motion planning* [41]. Furthermore, *multiplicative and additive weights* were associated with the points in S, that influence the distance to the other points in space [6,25]. For further references, the reader is referred to [23] and, in particular, to the survey on Voronoi diagrams by Aurenhammer [7].

Solving proximity problems, the underlying distance measure depends on the environment. For example, the distance between two points, $a = (a_1, a_2)$ and $b = (b_1, b_2)$, in a VLSI circuit layout (or in midtown Manhattan) must be measured in the metric L_1 of the family of Minkowski metrics $L_p(a, b) = (|a_1 - b_1|^p + |a_2 - b_2|^p)^{1/p}$, because only such paths between a and b are allowed that consist of segments parallel to the x-or to the y-axis (see Figure 1.8). Algorithms for constructing the Voronoi diagram in the L_1-metric were presented in [30,40], and for general L_p-metrics in [38]; the results on L_1 were generalized in [60] to the case where the segments of the paths may be parallel to a line out of a fixed, finite set. At the same time, an algorithm for the class of *convex distance functions* (cf. Section 1.2) was proposed in [14]. This class includes all *norms* in the plane and, thus, all the cases studied before. Voronoi diagrams based on such functions can also be used in solving motion planning problems; see [1], for example. The paper [14] contains several novel ideas that are capable of even further generalization (see, for example, Claim 4 in the proof of Theorem 4.2.3). However, no proof is given why a straightforward adaption of the algorithm [56] is possible, considering the problems discussed in Subsection 3.4.1.

In many situations, convex distance functions do not provide us with an adequate distance measure. If there are obstacles in the plane [39,3], or, more generally, regions to whose interior different metrics apply (like the Central Park in Manhattan) [46,26], then the distance between two points is no longer invariant under translations, as in the case of convex distance functions. The same holds true for the much more complicated metric measuring distances in a big city, taking into account the street and subway nets, and the possibility of getting a taxi in a given neighborhood; this problem was raised in [57]. So far, Voronoi diagrams for metrics other than norms have only been studied in special cases [3].

In this book a unifying approach to the theory of Voronoi diagrams is proposed by introducing *abstract Voronoi diagrams* (Chapter 2). These are not based on the notions of sites and distance, but on the concept of *bisecting curves*. We start with a system of simple curves, $J(p,q)$, where $p \neq q$ range over a finite index set S. The curves are supposed to tend to infinity at both ends, and the intersection of any two of them should not have more than finitely many connected components. Such a curve bisects the plane into two unbounded "halfplanes", just as a straight line does. So, Voronoi regions $R(p,S)$ can be defined in the usual way, by intersecting halfplanes. Together they form an abstract Voronoi diagram (or AVD, for short). We do, however, not consider arbitrary systems of bisecting curves but assume that *the resulting Voronoi regions $R(p,S)$ are connected and cover the plane.*

Now the investigation has two objectives. First, we want to prove these properties to be fulfilled in many concrete situations, in order to make shure that the concept of abstract Voronoi diagrams does in fact lead to a unification of the theory. Second, we are interested in efficient algorithms for constructing abstract Voronoi diagrams, because such an algorithm provides us with a universal tool for efficiently computing all concrete Voronoi diagrams that are covered by the AVD concept. This emphasizes the practical importance of abstract Voronoi diagrams.

As for the first problem, in Chapter 1 we consider the class of all metrics d in the plane that share the following properties. The d-circles are bounded with respect to the Euclidean metric, d induces the Euclidean topology, and to any two different points, a and c, there exists a point $b \notin \{a,c\}$, "between" a and b such that

*)
$$d(a,c) = d(a,b) + d(b,c)$$

holds. The resulting metric space is complete, and, by Menger's *Verbindbarkeits-satz* [45], two points in the plane can be joined by an arc α such that equation *) holds for any three consecutive points, a, b, c of α (such arcs are sometimes called shortest paths in the metric d). Since the Voronoi regions with respect to a metric d are always *d-star-shaped*, they are *connected*. The bisector

$$B(p,q) = \{z; d(p,z) = d(q,z)\}$$

of two points needs not be a curve (it can be a region, as in L_1, cf. Figure 1.10); we propose a way of choosing a subset $J(a,b)$ of its boundary that allows the d-Voronoi diagram of a point set $S_0 = \{p_A, \ldots, p_n\}$ to be defined in such a way that the resulting n regions form a *partition of the plane*, without having to make assumptions about the "general position" of the points. The metric d is called *nice* if, in addition to the above properties, the sets $J(p,q)$ are *simple curves* the intersection of any two of which consists of only finitely many components.

Before attacking the problem of how to compute abstract Voronoi diagrams, we must know their structural properties. In Chapter 2, the local structure of an abstract Voronoi diagram is studied first. Then its structure as a planar graph can be derived. Some care must be taken because in this general set-up, the curves may touch each other in such a way that the contour of a region need not be a simple curve. Without such degeneracies, an abstract Voronoi diagram, if circumscribed with a simple closed curve, is a biconnected planar graph each of whose vertices is of degree ≥ 3, and each such graph can be obtained.

In abstract Voronoi diagrams, two curves, $J(p,q)$ and $J(p,r)$, can cross twice, in contradistinction to the Euclidean Voronoi diagram (two curves, $J(p,q)$ and $J(v,w)$, that are not associated with the same p can cross arbitrarily often). Chapter 3 shows that this more complex situation can also be handled by a divide-and-conquer algorithm. We prove that two abstract Voronoi diagrams, $V(L_0)$ and $V(R_0)$, resulting from a partition of S_0 into L_0 and R_0, can be merged within a number of steps proportional to $|S_0|$, provided that the bisector of L_0 and R_0 is *acyclic*. Here a single step can be one out of four elementary operations on bisecting curves (e.g., determining the first point of intersection in a given direction). Only these operations need to be implemented, in order to adapt the algorithm to a concrete situation.

In Chapter 4 we return to the class of nice metrics, and give sufficient criteria for a partition of the set S_0 to be acyclic. One of them assumes that the circles in the metric d are simply-connected. It implies, for example, that the Voronoi diagram based on the fan-shaped street layout of Moscow (or Karlsruhe) can be computed in optimal $O(n \log n)$ time, using linear space. Another sufficient condition generalizes the concept of supporting halfplanes known from convex sets. It holds for classes of metrics that are closed under a patch operation, which allows different metrics to be assigned to the regions of a (not necessarily rectangular) grid.

Chapter 1

Voronoi diagrams in nice metrics

In Section 1.1 we briefly recall the definition of the Euclidean Voronoi diagram, some of its applications in the solution of proximity problems, and the different worst-case optimal techniques known for its computation. Then we turn to non-Euclidean metrics in the plane. The goal of Section 1.2 is to present a definition of the Voronoi diagram for general metrics, and a definition of a class of "nice" metrics in the plane that is both interesting and tractable, as far as the computation of the Voronoi diagram is concerned. This needs a few facts from the theory of metric spaces that are given without proofs; a complete presentation can be found in [53]. Otherwise, the section is self-contained, with respect to the notions from topology used. The concept of *straight arcs* in a metric is discussed in detail (such arcs are also called "shortest" or "geodetic" in the literature; however, an intuitively shortest path need not be straight, as will be illustrated by examples).

Throughout this chapter, the Euclidean distance, $L_2(a, b)$, of points will be denoted by $|a - b|$. For a real-valued function, $g(n)$, of integer arguments, $O(g(n))$ denotes the class of all functions $f(n)$ of the same kind, such that $|f(n)| \leq C \cdot |g(n)|$ holds for a suitable constant C and all n sufficiently large.

1.1 The Euclidean Voronoi diagram

Let $S = \{p_1, \ldots, p_n\}$ be a set of n different points in the plane. For $p, q \in S, p \neq q$, let

$$
\begin{aligned}
B(p, q) &= \{z \in \Re^2; \quad |p - z| = |q - z|\} \\
D(p, q) &= \{z \in \Re^2; \quad |p - z| < |q - z|\}
\end{aligned}
$$

$B(p, q)$ is the perpendicular *bisector* of the line segment joining p with q; of the two halfplanes separated by $B(p, q)$, $D(p, q)$ is the one that contains p, see Figure 1.1, a). The set

$$D(p, S) = \bigcap_{\substack{q \in S \\ q \neq p}} D(p, q)$$

of all points z that are closer to p than to any other element of S is called *the (open) Voronoi region of p with respect to S*; see Figure 1.1, b). $D(p, S)$ is the interior of a convex, possibly unbounded polygon. The points on the contour of $D(p, S)$ are those that have more than one nearest neighbor in S, one of which is p.

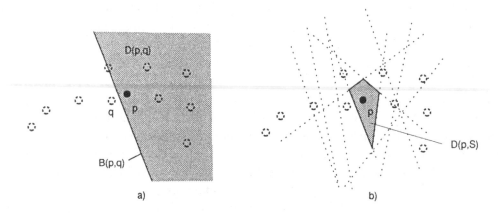

Figure 1.1: A Voronoi region.

The union

$$V(S) = \bigcup_{p \in S} \partial D(p, S)$$

of all region boundaries is called the *Voronoi diagram* of S; see Figure 1.2. The common boundary of two Voronoi regions is a *Voronoi edge*. Two edges meet at a *Voronoi vertex*; such a point has three or more nearest neighbors in the set S. In the example shown in Figure 1.1, b), only a few of the bisectors $B(p, q)$ actually contribute to the contour of $D(p, S)$. In fact, the total number of edges of $V(S)$ is only of order n.

Lemma 1.1.1 $V(S)$ *has only* $O(n)$ *many edges and vertices.*

Proof: (cf. [52,27], for example) By circumscribing a large enough "augmenting" curve, Γ, and cutting off the unbounded edges, $V(S)$ becomes an embedded planar graph with $n + 1$ faces. By the Euler Formula, we have

$$v - e + f \geq 2$$

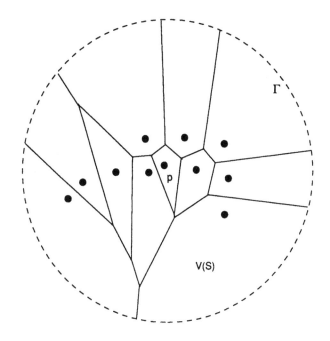

Figure 1.2: A Voronoi diagram with augmenting curve.

for the numbers of vertices, edges, and faces, correspondingly (here equality holds, since the graph is connected). At least three edges are outgoing from each vertex; thus $2e \geq 3v$ (because each edge is counted twice). This implies

$$v \leq 2n - 2$$
$$e \leq 3n - 3$$

$\square$

It also follows that a region contour consists of less than 6 edges, on the average. This suggests that constructing the Voronoi diagram by computing all of the n intersections of $n - 1$ halfplanes is too complicated. In fact, three algorithms have been introduced that allow the Euclidean Voronoi diagram of n points in the plane to be constructed within $O(n \log n)$ time and $O(n)$ storage, in the worst case. Either bound is asymptotically *worst case optimal* (n real numbers, $x_1, \ldots, x_n$, can be *sorted* by constructing the Voronoi diagram of $(x_1, 0), \ldots, (x_n, 0)$, and each sorting algorithm is known to require as many as $cn \log n$ steps for some constant c in the worst case [52]).

The first optimal algorithm, as given by Shamos and Hoey [56], made a divide-and-conquer approach. Here the problem of computing $V(S)$ is split into two

subproblems, namely to compute $V(L)$ and $V(R)$, where $S = L \cup R$ is a partition
into subsets of about equal size induced by a vertical (or horizontal) separating
line. $V(L)$ and $V(R)$ are computed recursively. Then the main task is in merging
the subdiagrams into $V(S)$; this step requires the computation of the "bisector"

$$B(L, R) = \{z \in \Re^2; \quad \min_{p \in L} |p - z| = \min_{q \in R} |q - z|\}$$

of the sets L and R, see Figure 1.3.

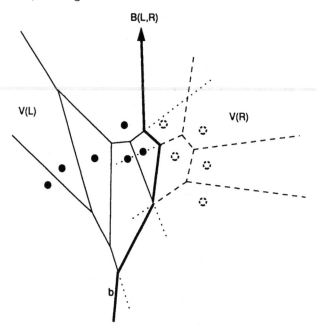

Figure 1.3: Merging $V(L)$ and $V(R)$.

A simpler description of $B(L, R)$ is that it consists of precisely those edges
of $V(S)$ that are common boundary of both an L-region and an R-region. The
algorithm first computes one of the two unbounded edges in $B(L, R)$, b. Then b
is traced until $V(L)$ or $V(R)$ is hit, whichever comes first. Next, the continuation
of b is determined. This way, $B(L, R)$ can be computed in time $O(n)$. The merge
step is completed by cutting off the excess parts of $V(L)$ and $V(R)$ marked by
dotted lines in Figure 1.3; this can even be done while $B(L, S)$ is traced. Due to
the $\log_2 n$ recursion depth, an overall performance of $O(n \log n)$ results. It is a
remarkable property of this algorithm that it *works on the system of bisectors and
does not have to evaluate distances*. This makes the divide-and-conquer algorithm
a natural candidate for generalization, as will be discussed in detail in Section 3.2.

The next optimal algorithm was introduced in [11]. Brown reduced the problem of constructing the Voronoi diagram of n points in Euclidean d-space to the construction of the *convex hull* of n points in $d + 1$-space. For $d = 2$, the points of S are mapped onto a sphere by stereographic projection. Three non-collinear points, p, q, and r, of S give rise to a Voronoi vertex (with adjacent regions of p, q, r) iff the circle, C, passing through p, q, and r contains no further point of S in its interior, see Figure 1.4. This is the case iff the plane H containing the mapped

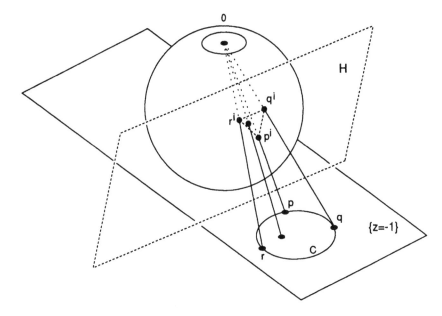

Figure 1.4: Stereographic projection.

images, p^i, q^i, and r^i, does *not* separate the pole, 0, from the other points of S^i (for, if the points of S are situated in the plane $\{z = -1\}$, and if 0 is the origin, the stereographic projection results from restricting the *inversion transform*

$$i : \Re^3 \longrightarrow \Re^3$$
$$a \longmapsto \frac{1}{|a|^2} \cdot a$$

to the plane $\{z = -1\}$. As any plane not containing 0, H is mapped by i onto a sphere K passing through 0, in such a way that the halfspace defined by H that does not contain 0 corresponds to the interior of K. Since $i^2 = \mathrm{id}$, it follows that $\{p, q, r\} \subset K$, hence $\{z = -1\} \cap K = C$). But this means that a) $\{p^i, q^i, r^i\}$ are lying on a face of the convex hull of S^i, and b) the convex hull lies on the same side of H as 0. Since the convex hull of n points in 3-space was already known to be computable in time $O(n \log n)$, this result allowed the Voronoi vertices to be determined and, thus, the 2-dimensional Voronoi diagram to be computed, within the same optimal time. This method also applies to higher dimensions; if $d \geq 3$ is odd then the maximum number of vertices a Voronoi diagram of n points can have is at least $\frac{1}{e}(\frac{d-1}{2})! n^{(d+1)/2}$ [32], whereas computation of the convex hull of n points in $d+1$-space can be accomplished within time $O(n^{(d+1)/2})$ [23]. A simpler way of transforming the problem into space of one higher dimension is described in [23]. Though these methods are most elegant, they seem less suitable for generalization to general metrics.

The third worst-case optimal algorithm was presented by Fortune [25]. It also uses a geometric transform, but for a different purpose. The objective was to bring the Voronoi diagram in such a form that a *sweep-line* technique can be employed to its computation. In the sweep-line approach, a horizontal line, l, is moved upward across the scene, and at each stage the set of "active" Voronoi edges currently intersected by l is maintained, in their left-to-right order. Whenever this set changes, the sweep-line must "halt", and the information stored about the active edges must be updated.

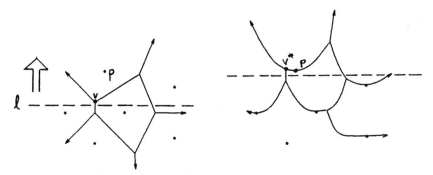

Figure 1.5: A Voronoi diagram bent by Fortune's transformation.

The problem is how to compute the halting points in time, that is, before the sweep-line has advanced too far. In the left picture shown in Figure 1.5 (as of [25]) the algorithm has no knowledge of the existence of vertex v, the next halting point, since it has not discovered the point p yet. After applying the transformation

$$* : a = (a_1, a_2) \longmapsto (a_1, a_2 + \min_{p \in S} |a - p|)$$

to the plane, this problem has disappeared: No point of the boundary of the transformed region, $D(p, S)^*$, lies below p (note that the elements of S are the fixed points of $*$). The map $*$ induces a deformation of $V(S)$ that does not change its structure. This is shown by proving that the order of points of $V(S)$ on a vertical line is preserved under $*$. The transformed diagram can now be computed within $O(n \log n)$ time, using the sweep-line method (there are $O(n)$ halting points, and each update of the set of active edges can be performed in time $O(\log n)$, using a suitable data structure). This approach would fail if it were necessary to compute all the transformed bisectors $B(p,q)^*$ in advance, which needs knowledge of $V(S)$. Fortunately, this is not the case. The algorithm can be run on the original bisectors; it needs to compute the mapping $*$ only for arguments where the minimum distance to the points in S is known. In addition, no retransforming is necessary, in order to obtain $V(S)$. A modified version of this algorithm avoids the transformation at all, and instead maintains the "beachline" bordering that part of the diagram below the sweepline that will not change any more, as the sweepline proceeds; see [16].

This algorithm is certainly the easiest one to implement. As to generalizations, in [25] also the cases of points with additive weights and straight line segments are settled. In [17] it was shown that the Voronoi diagram of points on a cone can be computed by a sweep-circle technique. Generalization to norms in the plane seems possible, more general metrics have apparently not yet been investigated (one potential hindrance rests in Proposition 2.2 not proven in [25]).

Once the Voronoi diagram of n points in the Euclidean plane has been constructed in time $O(n \log n)$, a number of important proximity problems can be solved within the same time bound.

If p, $q \in S$ are such that q is a nearest neighbor of p in S then the regions of p and q in $V(S)$ share an edge. Thus, the *all nearest neighbors* problem of finding to each point in S a nearest neighbor in S has an $O(n)$ reduction to the construction of $V(S)$. Similary, a *closest pair* in S^2 can be found.

The points on the *convex hull* of S are precisely those whose Voronoi region is unbounded (see [52], for example).

If no four points of S are cocircular then the planar dual of $V(S)$ [27], if realized by straight lines, is a triangulation of S [18]. This *Delaunay triangulation* is uniquely determined by the fact that the circle circumscribing a triangle does not contain a point of S in its interior. This, in turn, is equivalent to saying that the minimum angle of triangles is a maximum over all triangulations. The regularity of the triangles hereby ensured is useful in many applications (e.g., [55]).

Another proximity problem to whose solution the Voronoi diagram can contribute is the *nearest neighbor* or *post office problem* of finding a nearest neighbor in S to an arbitrary point, z, in the plane. In contradistinction to the above problems, z is a variable, whereas S remains fixed. Given $V(S)$, the problem reduces to determining an element p of S such that z belongs to (the closure of) $D(p, S)$. For this *point location* problem, various solutions are known. A solution that is time and space optimal under more general assumptions was given by Kirkpatrick [31]. After building up the Voronoi diagram, a search structure can be constructed in time $O(n \log n)$ that allows an arbitrary point z to be located within time $O(\log n)$. The whole structure has an $O(n)$ storage consumption.

1.2   Nice metrics

We are using the following standard notions from topology (cf. [22]). Let M be an arbitrary set. A *metric* on M is a mapping $d : M \times M \longrightarrow \Re_{\geq 0}$ such that for any elements a, b, and c of M the following conditions are fulfilled. One has

$$
\begin{aligned}
d(a, b) &= 0 & &\text{iff } a = b, \\
d(a, b) &= d(b, a) & &\text{(symmetry)}, \\
\text{and } d(a, c) &\leq d(a, b) + d(b, c) & &\text{(triangle inequality)}.
\end{aligned}
$$

(M, d) is then called a *metric space*, and $d(a, b)$ is the *distance* between a and b. The metric d induces a *topology* on M: a set $U \subset M$ is *open* if it contains with each element $a \in U$ a *d-ball*

$$
B_d(a, \epsilon) = \{z \in M; \ d(a, z) \leq \epsilon\}
$$

for $\epsilon > 0$ sufficiently small. From now on, only balls with a positive radius are considered. The complement, U^c, of an open set U is *closed*. The *boundary*, ∂A, of a set $A \subset M$ consists of those points $a \in A$ such that any ball $B_d(a, \epsilon)$ centered at a contains elements of both A and A^c. The union of A and ∂A is closed; it is called the *closure of* A, and denoted by $\overline{A}$. One has $A = \overline{A}$ iff A is closed. The set $A - \partial A$ is open; it is called the *interior* of A, and denoted by $\mathring{A}$. $A = \mathring{A}$ holds iff A itself is open. A sequence of elements, (a_n), of M *converges* to a iff $d(a_n, a)$ converges to 0 in $\Re$.

Two different metrics, d_1, and d_2, can induce the same topology on M. This is the case iff each d_1-ball contains a d_2-ball with the same center, and conversely. Roughly, if d_1 and d_2 induce the same topology then "closeness" means the same in either metric, but no way of comparing distances is implied.

In real k-space, points can be considered vectors. So, a measure of the distance of two points can be based on a measure of the length of the connecting vector.

Such a length measure is given by a *norm*

$$
\begin{array}{rcll}
N & : & \Re^k \longrightarrow \Re_{\geq 0} & \text{satisfying } N(a) = 0 \text{ iff } a = 0 \\
N(a + b) & \leq & N(a) + N(b) & \text{(triangle inequality), and} \\
N(\lambda a) & = & |\lambda| \cdot N(a) & \text{for any vectors } a, b \text{ in} \\
& & & k\text{-space and real numbers } \lambda
\end{array}
$$

Well known among the norms on $\Re^k$ is the family $\{L_p;\ p \geq 1\}$ where

$$
L_p((a_1, \ldots, a_k)) = (\sum_{i=1}^{k} |a_i|^p)^{\frac{1}{p}}.
$$

Here L_2 is the standard Euclidean norm, $|\cdot|$, L_1 gives the "Manhattan" length $|a_1| + |a_2| + \ldots + |a_k|$, and for $p \longrightarrow \infty$ one obtains the maximum norm $L_\infty((a_1, \ldots, a_k)) = \max_{1 \leq i \leq k} |a_i|$. Any two norms, N_1 and N_2, on $\Re^k$ are *equivalent*, in that

$$
cN_2(a) \leq N_1(a) \leq C N_2(a)
$$

holds for suitable constants $c, C > 0$, and arbitrary vectors a (cf. [8]). In particular, each norm induces the *Euclidean topology* on $\Re^k$.

Given a norm, N, a metric can be defined by $d(a, b) := N(a - b)$. Then the distance between a and b depends only on their relative position and is, thus, *invariant under translations*. Consequently,

$$
B_d(a, \epsilon) = a + B_d(0, \epsilon) = a + \epsilon B_d(0, 1)
$$

holds, the latter because of the third property of a norm. The unit ball $B_d(0, 1)$ has some nice properties; it is compact (=closed and bounded), symmetric to the origin (since $N(a) = N(-a)$) which is contained in its interior, and it is *convex*. Conversely, any such set, B, can be used for defining a norm, and thereby, a metric d such that $B_d(0, 1) = B$ holds (see [8]): to compute the distance between a and b, the set B is centered at a, and the (only) point of intersection, v, of the halfline radiating from a through b and the boundary of B is determined. Then

$$
d(a, b) = \frac{|a - b|}{|a - v|} \quad ,
$$

see Figure 1.6. If the set B is not symmetric to the origin, the function d obtained by this equation is not symmetric in a and b; such functions are called *convex distance functions*. The norms are precisely the symmetric convex distance functions. In Figure 1.7 the unit circles of the norms L_1, $L_2 = |\cdot|$, and L_∞ are depicted.

Those metrics on $\Re^k$ induced by norms can be characterized as follows.

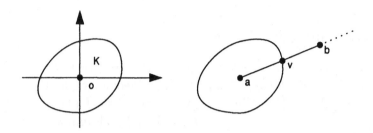

Figure 1.6: By $d(a,b) := |a - b|/|a - v|$ a convex distance function is defined.

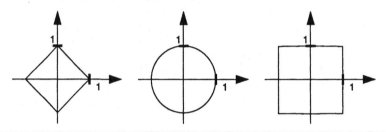

Figure 1.7: Unit circles of L_1, L_2, and L_∞.

Lemma 1.2.1 *A metric d on $\Re^k$ is induced by a norm iff it has the following properties.*

1. *d induces the Euclidean topology.*

2. *The d-distance is invariant under translations.*

3. *The d-distance is additive on straight lines (that is, if a, b, c are consecutive points on a straight line then $d(a, b) + d(b, c) = d(a, c)$ holds).*

Proof: Necessity is obvious, by the above. If d fulfills 1), 2), and 3), then by $N(a) := d(a, 0)$ a norm is defined. The triangle inequality for N is a consequence of 2). The equation $d(\lambda a, 0) = |\lambda| \, d(a, 0)$ is first shown for natural numbers λ by induction, using 3). It extends to rational numbers automatically, and from there to the reals by 1), and by the well-known continuity of a metric stated in the following lemma. □

Lemma 1.2.2 *If $(a_n) \longrightarrow a$ and $b_n \longrightarrow b$ hold for sequences (a_n), (b_n) in a metric space (M, d) then $d(a_n, b_n) \longrightarrow d(a, b)$ holds in $\Re$.*

Proof: (cf. [22]) We have $|d(a, b) - d(a_n, b_n)| \leq d(a, a_n) + d(b, b_n)$, by the triangle inequality. □

The first non-Euclidean metric in which Voronoi diagrams were studied was the "Manhattan" L_1-norm in the plane [30,40]. This research was motivated by the fact that in many environments only such motions are possible that are piecewise parallel to the x-or the y-axis. The minimum (Euclidean) length of such a path that joins a with b is given by $L_1(a,b)$, see Figure 1.8. In Figure 1.9 the L_1-Voronoi diagram of the four points is depicted, together with the Euclidean diagram. The

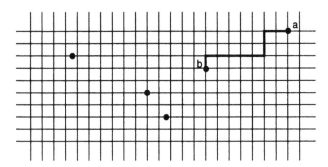

Figure 1.8: The Manhattan norm.

small example shows that the combinatorial structures are different. In the L_2-diagram, the regions of p and q are neighboring, whereas in the L_1-diagram they are not. The bisector of two points, p and q, in L_1 is a horizontal (a vertical) line iff p and q are lying on a vertical (a horizontal) line. If p and q are diagonal vertices of a non-degenerate rectangle then $B(p,q)$ consists of three line segments, unless the rectangle is a square. In this case, $B(p,q)$ consists of a line segment and two quarterplanes (see Figure 1.10) caused by the line segments in the boundary of the L_1-circle.

The problem of how the Voronoi diagram should be defined arises under these circumstances. Introducing additional Voronoi regions $R(T,S)$ consisting of all points whose nearest neighbors in S are precisely the points in $T \subset S$ would reflect proximity relations best; but this approach could result in a number of regions proportional to n^2 (Figure 1.12).

Instead, one wants to *choose a curve from $B(p,q)$* that separates p and q. Such a choice must be made in a consistent way or there will be points that are not contained in any Voronoi region (Figure 1.11).

For the L_1 norm, it has been suggested to choose the "clockwise most" boundary of $B(p,q)$ [40]; this is in fact how the bisector would look if the two points were slightly moved apart in the y-direction. In general, if the structure of the bisectors is not known, one must either make assumptions about the "general position" of the points in S, or employ a strategy for distributing the bisectors among the

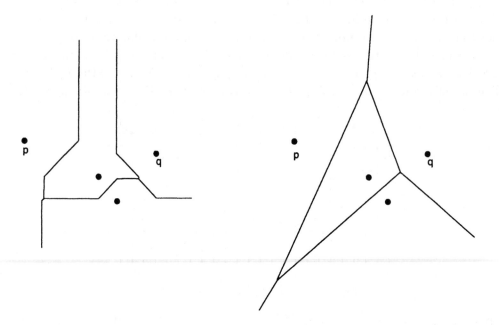

Figure 1.9: L_1 versus L_2.

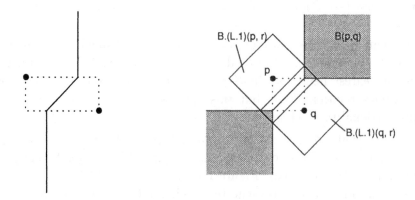

Figure 1.10: L_1-bisectors.

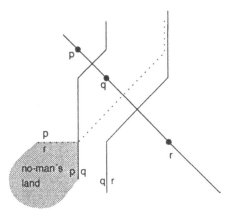

Figure 1.11: No-man's-land arising from a bad choice of bisecting curves.

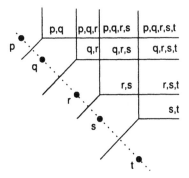

Figure 1.12: $\frac{(n-1)n}{2}$ bisector regions resulting from n points in L_1.

regions, as the following one.

Definition 1.2.3 Let (M, d) be a metric space, and assume that an order $\prec$ is given on M. Let $S \subset M$ be finite and non-empty. For points $p, q \in S$, $p \neq q$, let

$$R(p, q) := \begin{cases} C(p, q), & \text{if } p \prec q \\ D(p, q), & \text{if } q \prec p \end{cases}$$

where

$$\begin{aligned} C(p, q) &= \{z \in M; \quad d(p, z) \leq d(q, z)\} \\ D(p, q) &= \{z \in M; \quad d(p, z) < d(q, z)\}. \end{aligned}$$

Then

$$R(p, S) := \bigcap_{\substack{q \in S \\ q \neq p}} R(p, q)$$

is the *Voronoi region of p with respect to S*, and

$$V(S) := \bigcup_{p \in S} \partial R(p, S)$$

is the *Voronoi diagram of S*.

Clearly, the above definition depends on the order, $\prec$, on M; in the Euclidean case, however, any choice of $\prec$ leads to the same set $V(S)$. In the following, the metric space (M, d) and the order $\prec$ are fixed.

Lemma 1.2.4 *The regions $R(p, S)$ form a partition of M. $R(p, S)$ contains all points of M that are closer to p than to any other point in S. If $z \in \overline{R(p, S)}$ then p is a nearest neighbor of z in S.*

Proof: If $p \neq q$ then $R(p, S) \cap R(q, S) \subset R(p, q) \cap R(q, p) = \emptyset$, so the regions are pairwise disjoint. Now let $z \in M$, and let p be the minimum with respect to $\prec$ of the nearest neighbors of z in S. Then z belongs to $B(p, q) \subset R(p, q)$ for each nearest neighbor q in S different from p, and to $D(p, q) \subset R(p, q)$ if $d(p, z) < d(q, z)$ holds. Hence, $z \in R(p, S)$. Conversely, if $z \in \overline{R(p, S)}$ then a sequence $z_n \longrightarrow z$ exists, where $z_n \in R(p, S)$. From $d(p, z_n) \leq d(q, z_n)$ one obtains $d(p, z) \leq d(q, z)$, by continuity (Lemma 1.2.2). $\qquad \square$

In the Euclidean Voronoi diagram of points, the regions are convex. In particular, they are *star-shaped* in the following sense: If z belongs to the region of p then the line segment joining z with p is contained in the region of p, too. Chew and Drysdale [14] note that this property carries over to norms (whereas standard convexity fails to hold, e.g. in L_1). Aronov [3] correctly generalizes the concept of star-shapedness to the metric d defined by paths of a minimum Euclidean length inside a simple polygon; here the straight lines of the L_2-star-shapedness condition have to be replaced with minimum length paths. However, the further generalization to arbitrary metrics offered in [3] is not quite correct since it presupposes the existence of certain paths (the reference made to [52] seems erroneous).

In general, only a weaker condition holds for the Voronoi regions.

Definition 1.2.5 Let (M, d) be a metric space, and let $p \in A \subset M$. Then A is called *d-star-shaped, as seen from* p, iff it has the following property.

$$\forall a \in A \; \forall b \in M \; (d(p, a) = d(p, b) + d(b, a) \implies b \in A).$$

This is to say, if a belongs to A then each point metrically "between" p and a (one for which the triangle inequality becomes an equality) also does. Each d-sphere is d-star-shaped, as seen from its center. In L_2 the points "between" p and a are precisely those on the straight line segment connecting p and a. Therefore, a set is L_2-star-shaped iff it is star-shaped in the standard sense.

Lemma 1.2.6 *Each Voronoi region $R(p, S)$ is d-star-shaped, as seen from p.*

Proof: Since star-shapedness is stable in intersections, it suffices to show that the sets $D(p, q)$ and $C(p, q)$ of Definition 1.2.3 are star-shaped. Assume that $a \in D(p, q)$, $b \in M$, and $d(p, a) = d(p, b) + d(b, a)$ hold. If $b \notin D(p, q)$ then $d(q, b) \leq d(p, b)$, hence

$$d(q, a) \leq d(q, b) + d(b, a) \leq d(p, b) + d(b, a) = d(p, a)$$

contradicting $a \in D(p, q)$. The proof for $C(p, q)$ is analogous. □

This lemma is void if the only points b satisfying $d(p, a) = d(p, b) + d(b, a)$ are p and a themselves.

Example 1 By $d(a, c) := \sqrt{|a - c|}$ a metric is defined in the plane. Taking squares shows that

$$d(a, c) < d(a, b) + d(b, c)$$

holds, unless $|a - b||b - c| = 0$. Nonetheless, the d-Voronoi diagram is the Euclidean Voronoi diagram.

The next example is less artificial.

Example 2 Let f be a fixed point (a flowershop) in the plane. A person living at point a, who wants to visit someone else living at point c, first goes to f, to buy some flowers, see Figure 1.13 a). Thus,

$$d(a,c) = \begin{cases} |a-f| + |f-c| & \text{if } a \neq c \\ 0 & \text{if } a = c \end{cases}$$

If a, b, c are pairwise different then $d(a,c) < d(a,b) + d(b,c)$, unless $b = f$. Thus, no point other than a, f is between a and f (Figure b)). The topology induced is not the Euclidean topology; a Voronoi region may even collapse to a single point. Indeed, if $|p-f| < |q-f|$ for all q in S different from p, then $R(q,S) = \{q\}$, if $q \neq p$, and $R(p,S) = \Re^2 - (S - \{p\})$, see Figure c).

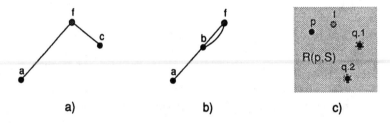

a)   b)   c)

Figure 1.13: The flowershop metric.

If $k > 1$ flowershops are available, one buys the flowers where the detour is a minimum. Thus, $d(a,b) = 0$ if $a = b$, and $d(a,b) = \min_{1 \leq i \leq k} |a - f_i| + |f_i - b|$, otherwise.

Theorem 1.2.7 *The Voronoi diagram of a set S of n points with respect to d can be computed in time $O(n \log n + k \log k)$ and space $O(n + k)$.*

Proof: Let z be a point in the plane, and let $p \neq z$ be a d-nearest neighbor of z in S. Assume that $d(p,z) = |p - f_i| + |f_i - z|$ holds. Then p is a Euclidean nearest neighbor of f_i in S. Otherwise, assume that $q \in S$ and $|q - f_i| < |p - f_i|$; then

$$d(q,z) \leq |q - f_i| + |f_i - z| < |p - f_i| + |f_i - z| = d(p,z),$$

a contradiction. Now we construct in $O(n \log n)$ time and $O(n)$ space the Euclidean Voronoi diagram of S, and build up a point location structure (as mentioned at the end of Section 1.1). Then, to each flowershop f_i a nearest neighbor p_i in S is determined (should there be more than one, the minimum with respect to a fixed order $\prec$ is taken), at a total cost of $O(k \log n)$. Let S' denote the set of sites p_i. If $p \in S - S'$ then $R(p,S) = \{p\}$, according to the above and to Definition 1.2.3, in case of ties. If $p \in S'$ then $R(p,S) = R(p,S') - (S - S')$. Let $w_i := |p_i - f_i|$ and

$d_i(z) = w_i + |f_i - z|$. Furthermore, let $D(f_i, f_j) = \{z; d_i(z) \le d_j(z)\}, i \ne j$, and similary for $C(f_i, f_j)$. Regions $R(f_i, F)$ can be defined as in Definition 1.2.3 (basing on any order among the f_i such that $f_i \prec f_j$ holds if $p_i \prec p_j$). This results in a *Euclidean Voronoi diagram of k points f_i with associated additive weights w_i*. Such a diagram can be computed in time $O(k \log k)$ and space $O(k)$, using Fortune's sweep-line algorithm, as described in [25]. The assertion follows because the region of p with respect to S' is just the union of all regions $R(f_i, F)$ where $p_i = p$. $\square$

The above examples show that an arbitrary metric need not admit points between a and c that are different from a and c; in this case, Lemma 1.2.6 is meaningless. We will not study such metrics any further.

Definition 1.2.8 An *arc* π in (M, d) is called *d-straight* if for any consecutive points a, b, and c of π the equality $d(a, c) = d(a, b) + d(b, c)$ holds.

By an *arc* π we mean the mapped image of the closed interval $[0, 1]$ under a continuous injective map $f : [0, 1] \longrightarrow M$, which is called a *parametrization* of π. The map f induces an order among the points on π; if a, $b \in \pi$ then $a < b$ iff $f^{-1}(a) < f^{-1}(b)$ holds for the unique inverse images in $[0, 1]$. Clearly, if a and c are on a *d*-straight arc then plenty of points b exist "between" them. *Thus, d-straight arcs do not exist in the above example metrics.*

Theorem 1.2.9 *(Menger [45], 1928) Let (M, d) be a complete metric space, and assume that to any two different points, a and c, a point $b \notin \{a, c\}$ exists such that $d(a, c) = d(a, b) + d(b, c)$ holds. Then two points of M can always be joined by a d-straight arc in M.*

(M, d) is *complete* iff each *d*-Cauchy sequence in M has a limit in M. A proof of Menger's *Verbindbarkeitssatz*, and a detailed presentation of the concepts of length and straightness, as well as of the "between" relation, can be found in [53]. If (M, d) is a metric space then the *d*-length, $\lambda_d(\pi)$, of an arc π can be defined, intuitively by adding up *d*-distances of consecutive points of π, making the resolution arbitrarily fine. By

$$d_i(a, b) := \inf_\pi \lambda_d(\pi),$$

the infimum taken over all arcs π that join a with b, a second metric is defined on M. In general, only $d_i(a, b) \ge d(a, b)$ holds true, but if a *d-straight arc* π connecting a and b exists then $\lambda_d(\pi) = d(a, b) = d_i(a, b)$. Thus, under the assumptions of the theorem, the distance of a and b equals the minimum *d*-length of all arcs connecting a with b, and the minimum is taken precisely by the *d*-straight arcs.

For this reason, d-straight arcs are sometimes called *d-shortest*, but one should be careful not to confuse this concept with the arcs that have possibly been used in *defining* the metric d. For example, the distance between a and b in the (single) flowershop metric can be defined as the minimum Euclidean length of all arcs that lead from a and b and visit f; but no straight arc exists in this metric. Sufficient conditions for a metric defined by arcs not to behave in this manner are given in §16, [53].

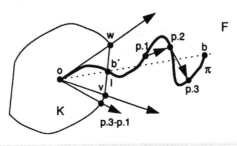

Figure 1.14: Not a d-straight arc.

Theorem 1.2.9 holds for all metrics on $\Re^k$ that are induced by *norms*. Here the straight arcs can easily be characterized. To give an example, we consider the planar case. Since length is invariant under translations, it suffices to determine the straight arcs with endpoint 0. We already know from Lemma 1.2.1 that the common straight line segments are d-straight. Let $K = B_d(0,1)$ be the unit circle, and for a point $b \neq 0$ let b' denote the unique point where the halfline radiating from 0 to b intersects the boundary of K.

Theorem 1.2.10 *Let d be induced by a norm on $\Re^2$. For $b \neq 0$, let l be the maximal line segment of ∂K containing b', and let v, w be the endpoints of l. If $v = w$ then the straight line segment $\overline{0b}$ is the only d-straight arc from 0 to b. If $v \neq w$ then an arc from 0 to b is d-straight iff both its v-and its w-coordinate functions are non-decreasing; see Figure 1.14.*

Proof: Assume that $d(a,b) = N(a - b)$, where N is a norm on $\Re^2$. If c and d are not collinear with 0 then $N(c + d) = N(c) + N(d)$ holds iff K is "as small as possible" in direction of $c + d$, i.e. iff the contour of K is a line segment between c' and d', see Figure 1.15 (for, the point s where the line through 0 and $c + d$ intersects the segment $\overline{c'd'}$ must be of norm 1, hence on ∂K; see [8]). Now let b, b', l, v, w be as in the theorem. Assume $v \neq w$ (the case $v = w$ is simpler). Since 0 lies in the interior of K, v and w are not collinear with 0. Let

$$F = \{\lambda v + \mu w; \quad \lambda \geq 0 \ \& \ \mu \geq 0\}$$

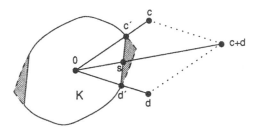

Figure 1.15: $N(c+d) = N(c) + N(d)$ holds iff the shaded areas do not belong to K.

be the first quadrant in the (v, w) coordinate system. By the above,

*) $\qquad c + d \in F \ \& \ N(c+d) = N(c) + N(d) \Longleftrightarrow c \in F \ \& \ d \in F$

holds for arbitrary c and d, because l was assumed to be maximal. Let π be an arc from 0 to $b \in F$ with parametrization $(v(t), w(t))$, $0 \le t \le 1$, and let $p_i = (v(t_i), w(t_i))$ for $t_1 < t_2 < t_3$. If both $v(t)$ and $w(t)$ are non-decreasing functions of t then $p_2 - p_1 \in F$ and $p_3 - p_2 \in F$, and the straightness condition for p_1, p_2, p_3 follows from *). Conversely, assume that π is d-straight. By the above equivalence, $p_3 - p_1 \in F$ implies $p_2 - p_1 \in F$ and $p_3 - p_2 \in F$, if p_1, p_2, p_3 are consecutive. If two consecutive points, q and r, of π are given, this implication yields $b - q \in F$ when applied to $(p_1, p_2, p_3) = (0, q, b)$, and another application, to (q, r, b), gives $r - q \in F$. Hence, the coordinates of π do not decrease from q to r. $\square$

Theorem 1.2.10 generalizes a result of [60] on norms defined by symmetric convex $2n$-gons.

Corollary 1.2.11 *If d is induced by a norm in the plane then the following assertions are equivalent.*
1. No three points of $\partial B_d(0, 1)$ are collinear.
2. The only d-straight arcs are the straight line segments.
3. The bisectors $B(p, q)$, $p \ne q$, have no interior.

Proof: 1) $\Longleftrightarrow$ 2) follows from the theorem. 3) $\Longrightarrow$ 1) is evident (see Figure 1.10). 2) $\Longrightarrow$ 3): by contradiction. Assume that $B_d(t, \epsilon) \subset B(p, q)$, and let $z \in B_d(t, \epsilon)$ be a point different from t on the straight line segment $\overline{pt}$ (Figure 1.16). Then $d(q, z) + d(z, t) = d(p, z) + d(z, t) = d(p, t) = d(q, t)$. Thus, z is between q and t, which implies that the concatenation of a d-straight arc π_1 from q to z

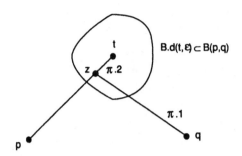

Figure 1.16: An illustration of the proof of 1.2.11.

and of a d-straight arc π_2 from z to t results again in a d-straight arc (cf. 3., §18, in [53]). For, one has $\lambda_d(\pi_1 \circ \pi_2) = \lambda_d(\pi_1) + \lambda_d(\pi_2) = d(q,z) + d(z,t) = d(q,t)$. Due to 2), the concatenation of $\overline{qz}$ and $\overline{zt}$ must be a straight line segment. This is only possible if $p = q$, a contradiction.   □

In many situations, a metric induced by a norm does not provide us with a realistic distance measure, because the invariance of distance under translations is not granted; examples are shown in Figure 1.17. Therefore, we make the following definition. Let $\prec$ denote a fixed order on $\Re^2$ (the lexicographic order, for example).

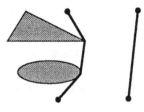 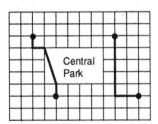

Figure 1.17: Examples of metrics where the distance between two points depends not only on their relative positions.

Definition 1.2.12 (Klein/Wood) A metric d on $\Re^2$ is called *nice* if it enjoys the following properties.

1. d induces the Euclidean topology.

2. The d-circles are bounded with respect to the Euclidean metric.

3. If $a, c \in \Re^2$ and $a \neq c$ then there exists a point $b \notin \{a,c\}$ such that $d(a,c) = d(a,b) + d(b,c)$ holds.

4. If $p, q \in \Re^2$ and $p \prec q$ then $J(p, q) := C(p, q) \cap \overline{D(p, q)}$ is a curve homeomorphic to $(0, 1)$. The intersection of two such curves, $J(p, q)$ and $J(v, w)$, consists of finitely many connected components.

Here $C(p, q)$ and $D(q, p)$ are as defined in 1.2.3. By definition, $J(p, q)$ is closed, as a set. Thus, if $f : (0, 1) \longrightarrow J(p, q)$ is a homeomorphism (i.e. one-to-one and bicontinuous) then $\lim_{t \to \pm \infty} |f(t)| = \infty$. (For, if $t_n \to \infty$ and $|f(t_n)| < C$ for all n, then the infinite set $\{f(t_n); n \geq 1\}$ would be bounded and would, by the Bolzano-Weierstrass Theorem, have an accumulation point, z, such that for a subsequence (t_{n_k}) of (t_n) $f(t_{n_k}) \to z$ holds. But $J(p, q)$ is closed, hence $z = f(t)$ where $t \in (0, 1)$, Since the inverse of f is continuous, $t_{n_k} \to t$ follows, in contradiction to $t_n \to \infty$). By applying stereographic projection, $J(p, q)$ becomes a simple closed curve on the sphere that passes through the pole. Clearly, $J(p, q) \subseteq B(p, q)$ holds.

Each metric induced by a norm fulfills 1), 2), and 3). Property 2) means that the metric d is continuous at infinity with respect to the Euclidean metric. The additional property 4) is of a mere technical nature; it is to ensure that the boundaries of the Voronoi diagrams are curves (otherwise, it would not be clear how to represent a Voronoi diagram), and that not too many intersections exist in a neighborhood of a point, or at infinity (otherwise, the local analysis done in Section 2.3 would be hindered).

Nice metrics have nice Voronoi diagrams; we summarize as follows.

Theorem 1.2.13 *Let d be nice, and let $V(S)$ be the Voronoi diagram of a finite set $S \subset \Re^2$ with respect to d. Then each region $R(p, S)$ is a path-connected set with a non-empty interior. It contains all points of the plane that are closer (with respect to d) to p than to any other point in S. Its closure consists of points that have p as a nearest neighbor in S. The system of regions $R(p, S)$ forms a partition of the plane.*

Proof: By 1) and 2), $(\Re^2, d)$ is complete (using the theorem by Bolzano and Weierstrass). By Theorem 1.2.9, any two points can be joined by a d-straight arc, π. If p and $z \in R(p, S)$ are joined by π then $\pi \subset R(p, S)$, as a consequence of Lemma 1.2.6. If ϵ is sufficiently small then each point of $B_d(p, \epsilon)$ is closer (in d) to p than to any other point in S; thus

$$B_d(p, \epsilon) \subset \bigcap_{\substack{q \in S \\ q \neq p}} D(p, q) \subset R(p, S)$$

holds, showing that p belongs to the interior of $R(p, S)$. The rest follows from Definition 1.2.3 and Lemma 1.2.4. □

Chapter 2

Abstract Voronoi diagrams

Given a finite set, S, of points in the Euclidean plane, the Voronoi region of a point p in S equals the intersection of all halfplanes $D(p, q)$ containing p that arise from the bisectors

$$B(p, q) = \{z \in \Re^2; |p - z| = |q - z|\}$$

where $q \in S$ is different from p. An analogous definition is possible if an arbitrary metric, d, is considered, provided that the bisectors with respect to d are still curves bisecting the plane.

In this chapter we introduce the concept of *abstract Voronoi diagrams* that are not based on a distance measure but on systems of simple curves, $J(p, q)$, that bisect the plane, as primary objects. It will be required that the two domains separated by such a curve are unbounded, and that the *Voronoi regions* defined by analogy with the above form a partition of the plane into path-connected sets with non-empty interiors. The *Voronoi diagram*, $V(S)$, is defined to be the union of the region boundaries.

As we shall see in Chapter 3, these assumptions are strong enough to make a generalization of the *scan principle* work, the very core of the algorithm first used by Shamos and Hoey [56] for computing Euclidean Voronoi diagrams; it is not necessary to assume that the regions are convex. On the other hand, the results of Chapter 1 show that the bisector system of a nice metric does have the properties required.

The points on the bisecting curves are distributed among the Voronoi regions, in order to obtain a partition of the plane. Ties resulting from intersections of several curves are broken by assuming that a fixed global ordering is given among the regions; a point contained in the common boundary of two regions or more belongs to the minimal one among them. Since we do not forbid these bisecting curves to touch one another, a region boundary needs not be simple. Instead, a region can contain "thin" parts consisting of cut-points (i.e., points whose removal leaves the region disconnected). Thus, the graph structure underlying the region boundaries differs from $V(S)$ (cf. Figure 2.19).

In order to obtain the structure of the planar graph, $\widehat{V}(S)$, behind the set $V(S)$ we first investigate the neighborhoods of the points in $V(S)$ (Section 2.3). This local information is then put together to derive the shape of the Voronoi regions (Section 2.5) as well as to define the graph $\widehat{V}(S)$ (Section 2.6). Rather than dealing with unbounded edges we shall assume that the system of bisecting curves is augmented by a simple closed curve large enough to encircle the interesting part of the Voronoi diagram (Section 2.4). In Section 2.7 the structure of those planar graphs is characterized that arise from abstract Voronoi diagrams. This section is independent of the rest of this paper.

2.1   Definitions

Throughout this chapter, a subset J of the plane is called a *bisecting curve* iff J is homeomorphic to the open interval $(0,1)$ and closed as a subset of $\Re^2$. By the Jordan Curve Theorem (see [54], for example) J dissects the plane into two unbounded domains each of which has J as its complete boundary.

Now let $n \in \mathcal{N}$, and for each pair of integers p, q such that $1 \le p \ne q \le n$ let $J(p,q) = J(q,p)$ be a bisecting curve. Let $D(p,q)$ and $D(q,p)$ denote the two domains separated by $J(p,q)$. We shall assume that for each curve $J(p,q)$ the choice has been made which one of the two domains is $D(p,q)$. By analogy with concrete Voronoi diagrams we define the *abstract Voronoi diagram* as follows.

Definition 2.1.1 Let $S := \{1, \ldots, n\}$ and

$$
\begin{aligned}
R(p,q) : \ &= \ \begin{cases} D(p,q) \cup J(p,q), & \text{if } p < q \\ D(p,q), & \text{if } p > q \end{cases} \\
R(p,S) : \ &= \ \bigcap_{\substack{q \in S \\ q \ne p}} R(p,q) \qquad \text{(Voronoi region of } p \text{ w.r.t. } S\text{).} \\
V(S) : \ &= \ \bigcup_{p \in S} \partial R(p,S) \qquad \text{(Voronoi diagram of } S\text{).}
\end{aligned}
$$

(In the "real" case, where a metric d is given, we have defined $R(p,q) = C(p,q)$, if $p < q$ (Definition 1.2.3), and $J(p,q) = C(p,q) \cap \overline{D(p,q)}$ (Definition 1.2.12), where C and D are defined in terms of d. Then the domain on the p-side of $J(p,q)$ equals $C(p,q) - J(p,q)$, whereas the domain on the q-side is $D(q,p)$. Clearly, Definition 2.1.1 yields the same regions and the same diagram; but the meaning of $D(p,q)$ can be different if $p < q$). We will be concerned only with such systems of bisecting curves that have the following properties.

Definition 2.1.2 A system of bisecting curves $(S, \{J(p,q); p,q \in S, p \neq q\})$ is called *admissible* iff the following conditions are fulfilled.

1. The intersection of any two bisecting curves consists of finitely many connected components.

2. For each non-empty subset S' of S

   A) $R(p, S')$ is path-connected and has a non-empty interior, for each $p \in S'$.

   B) $\Re^2 = \bigcup_{p \in S'} R(p, S')$ (disjoint).

It follows from Theorem 1.2.13 that the bisector system of a nice metric is admissible. *We will frequently assume that a fixed point, denoted by p, has been chosen from the interior of each region $R(p, S)$, such that each curve $J(p, q)$ can be considered as a curve separating p from q.* These points will often be referred to as sites.

It will be shown in Lemma 3.5.1.1 that it is sufficient to claim property *B)* of the above definition for all subsets S' of size 3. The connectedness assumption *A)* imposes restrictions on how two bisecting curves, $J(p, q)$ and $J(p, r)$, that belong to the same site p, can intersect; see Lemma 3.5.2.5.

Examples. Figure 2.1 displays a system of bisecting curves that is not admissible because the points of the bounded domain belong to none of the regions, thereby violating condition *B)*. The system shown in Figure 2.2 is admissible iff $p = \min\{p, q, r\}$, because only then does the segment T belong to $R(p, \{p, q, r\})$ and provide the required connecting arc between the two shaded subsets of this region.

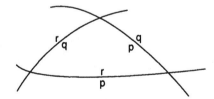

Figure 2.1: A system that is not admissible.

Suppose that $p < q, r$ holds in the example depicted in Figure 2.2. Then the planar graph underlying $V(\{p, q, r\})$ is not the one shown in Figure 2.3, a) which would not reflect the fact that the region of p is connected, but the one

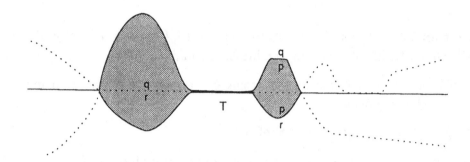

Figure 2.2: An admissible system iff $p < q, r$.

displayed in Figure 2.3, b). In Section 2.6 we show how to define in a systematic way the proper graph structure that underlies the set $V(S)$. *For the rest of this section we assume that $(S, \{J(p,q); p,q \in S$ and $p \neq q\})$ is a fixed admissible system of bisecting curves.* In Section 2.4 this concept will be slightly modified by introducing *augmented curve systems*.

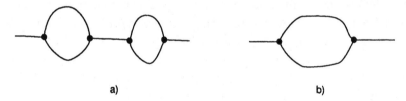

a)   b)

Figure 2.3: Only the right graph meets Figure 2.2.

2.2   Elementary properties

In this section some simple properties of the set $V(S)$ are listed that will be needed in Section 2.3 in proving that each sufficiently small neigborhood of a point $v \in V(S)$ looks as one might expect intuitively: a pie consisting of two pieces or more, each piece belonging to one of the regions $R(p, S)$, and some of them possibly thin as a curve. The reader who is willing to accept this without proof may read Lemma 2.2.4, Definition 2.3.4, and then continue with Theorem 2.3.5.

Lemma 2.2.1 *Let $p, q \in S$, $p \neq q$.*

1. $\overline{R(p,S)} \cap \overline{R(q,S)} \subseteq J(p,q)$.

2. $R(p, S) \cap \overline{R(q, S)} \neq \emptyset \Longrightarrow p < q.$

3. $V(S) = \bigcup_{\substack{p,q,\in S \\ p<q}} R(p, S) \cap \overline{R(q, S)} = \bigcup_{\substack{p,q,\in S \\ p<q}} R(p, S) \cap J(p, q).$

Proof:
1) $\overline{R(p, S)} \cap \overline{R(q, S)} \subseteq \overline{R(p, q)} \cap \overline{R(q, p)} = J(p, q).$
2) $\emptyset \neq R(p, S) \cap \overline{R(q, S)} \subseteq R(p, q) \cap \overline{R(q, p)}$ implies $J(p, q) \subset R(p, q)$, which in turn yields $p < q$.
3) Let $v \in \partial R(p, S) \subseteq V(S)$; since S is finite, there exists $q \in S$, $q \neq p$, such that each neighborhood of v contains a point of $R(q, S)$. Thus, $v \in \overline{R(p, S)} \cap \overline{R(q, S)}$. Because of Definition 2.1.2, $B)$, v is contained in a region $R(r, S)$. If $r \neq q$ then, by 2), $r < q$ and $v \in R(r, S) \cap \overline{R(q, S)} \subseteq R(r, S) \cap J(r, q)$, according to 1). To prove the converse, let $v \in R(p, S) \cap J(p, q)$, where $p < q$; since $J(p, q) \subset \overline{R(q, p)}$, v cannot belong to the interior of $R(p, S) \subseteq R(p, q)$. Hence, $v \in \partial R(p, S) \subseteq V(S)$.
$\square$

Lemma 2.2.2 *Let α be an arc joining a with b, and let α_0 denote the "open" curve α without its endpoints. Let us assume that $\alpha_0 \cap R(p, S) \cap \overline{R(q, S)} \neq \emptyset$ implies $\alpha_0 \subset J(p, q)$, for arbitrary p, $q \in S$. Then there exists an $r \in S$ such that $\alpha_0 \subset R(r, S)$.*

Proof: By contradiction. The points on α are linearly ordered. Suppose there exist s, u on α such that $a < s < u < b$ and $s \in R(p, S)$, $u \notin R(p, S)$. Let

$$t := \sup(\{z \in \alpha \; ; \; s \leq z \leq u\} \cap R(p, S)).$$

Clearly, $t \in [s, u] \subset \alpha_0$ and $t \in \overline{R(p, S)}$. If $t \notin R(p, S)$ then $t \in R(q, S)$, hence $q < p$ by Lemma 2.2.1, 2), and $\alpha_0 \subset J(q, p) \subset R(q, p)$ by assumption. This contradicts $s \in \alpha_0 \cap R(p, S)$. If $t \in R(p, S)$ then $t < u$; because S is finite there must exist a point $q \in S$ and a sequence of points $z_n \in R(q, S)$ such that $t < z_n \leq u$ on α_0 and $\lim_n z_n = t$. Thus, $t \in R(p, S) \cap \overline{R(q, S)}$, hence $p < q$ and $\alpha_0 \subset J(p, q) \subset R(p, q)$, in contradiction to $z_1 \in \alpha_0 \cap R(q, S)$.
$\square$

From the latter lemma we obtain the following separation result.

Corollary 2.2.3 *Let α be an arc joining $a \in R(p, S)$ with $b \in R(q, S)$, where $p \neq q$. Then $\alpha \cap V(S) \neq \emptyset$.*

Proof: Let $\alpha_0 := \alpha - \{a, b\}$. If $\alpha_0 \subset R(r, S)$ for a site $r \in S$ then $r \neq p$ or $r \neq q$. Assume $r \neq p$; then $a \in \alpha$ belongs to $R(p, S) \cap \overline{R(r, S)} \subset V(S)$. If α_0 is not entirely contained in one region then the above lemma implies the existence of two sites, p and q, in S such that $\emptyset \neq \alpha_0 \cap R(p, S) \cap \overline{R(q, S)} \subset V(S)$.   □

The following lemma shows that the Voronoi regions do not contain holes, i.e. that they are simply-connected.

Lemma 2.2.4 *Let $C \subset \overline{R(p, S)}$ be a closed curve. Then each of the bounded domains separated by C is contained in $R(p, S)$.*

Proof: The complement of C consists of disjoint domains exactly one of which, D_∞, is unbounded ([22], Chap. XVII, Theorem 1.2). Let D be one of the bounded domains. If $D \not\subset R(p, S)$ there is a point z in D such that $z \in R(q, S) \subseteq R(q, p)$ and $C \subset \overline{R(p, S)} \subseteq \overline{R(p, q)}$ hold, where $q \neq p$. Since D is open, we may assume $z \in D(q, p)$ (if $z \in J(p, q)$ then each neighborhood contains elements of $D(q, p)$). The unbounded domain $D(q, p)$ can't be contained in a bounded set ; thus, there exists a point $z' \in D(q, p)$ in D_∞. Let α be an arc in $D(q, p)$ connecting z with z'. Because $z \in D, z' \in D_\infty, \alpha$ must meet C, contradicting $D(q, p) \cap C = \emptyset$; see Figure 2.4.   □

Remark 2.2.5 By Lemma 2.2.4, $V(S)$ cannot be a bounded set if S contains at least two points.

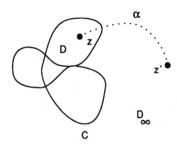

Figure 2.4: An illustration of the proof of Lemma 2.2.4.

2.3   The neighborhoods of points in V(S)

We will need the following technical result as a tool. As usual, let

$$U_\epsilon(v) = \{z \in \Re^2; \ |z - v| < \epsilon\}$$

denote the open disc of radius ϵ centered at v.

Lemma 2.3.1 *Let $\alpha_1, \ldots, \alpha_m$ be arcs in $\Re^2$ leading from a common point v to points $p_1, \ldots, p_m$, respectively, such that $\alpha_j \cap \alpha_k = \{v\}$ holds if $j \neq k$. Then for each $\epsilon > 0$ there exists a domain D such that*

1. $v \in D \subseteq U_\epsilon(v)$.

2. ∂D is a simple closed curve.

3. $\partial D \cap \alpha_j$ consists of exactly one point $(1 \leq j \leq m)$.

Proof: See [54], 40.20. The proof given there implicitly uses the Jordan-Schoenfliess Theorem. An easier proof can be based on [49], Chap. VI, Theorem 14.6. □

If the α_j are known to be piecewise smooth it is not hard to see that D can be chosen as $U_\epsilon(v)$.

Now let v be a point in $V(S)$, and let $S' = \{p_1, \ldots, p_m\}$ denote the set of all points $p \in S$ such that $v \in \overline{R(p, S)}$. By Lemma 2.2.1 we obtain

- $m \geq 2$

- $v \in J(p, q)$ if $p, q \in S', p \neq q$ *)

- $v \in R(p_\mu, S)$ where $p_\mu := \min S'$.

Since S is finite one can find $\eta > 0$ such that each neighborhood $U \subseteq U_\eta(v)$ of v has the following properties.

- $p \in S$ and $\overline{R(p, S)} \cap U \neq \emptyset \Longleftrightarrow p \in S'$

- $p, q \in S$ and $J(p, q) \cap U \neq \emptyset \Longrightarrow v \in J(p, q)$ **)

- $p, q, r, s \in S$, $w \in U$, and $v, w \in J(p, q) \cap J(r, s) \Longrightarrow J(p, q)$ and $J(r, s)$ coincide between v and w.

For the latter we have used the finiteness assumption of Definition 2.1.2. Each curve $J(p, q)$ passing v is split into two segments radiating from v that tend to infinity. By decreasing η further we can assure that any two such segments that have a point $w \in U_\eta(v) - \{v\}$ in common coincide before they meet $\partial U_\eta(v)$ first. This way, each bisecting curve through v gives rise to two arcs joining v with points of the boundary of $U_\eta(v)$ such that arcs arising from different curves have either only v in common, or coincide. Now let $\epsilon > 0$ be so small that all the prolongations of these arcs stay outside $U_\epsilon(v)$. An application of Lemma 2.3.1 yields

Lemma 2.3.2 *For each point $v \in V(S)$ there exist arbitrarily small neighborhoods U such that*

- *∂U is a simple closed curve.*

- *each bisecting curve $J(p,q)$ meeting U contains v and is cut by v into two curve segments each of which intersects ∂U exactly once.*

- *inside $\overline{U}$, any two such curve segments have either only the point v in common, or they coincide completely.*

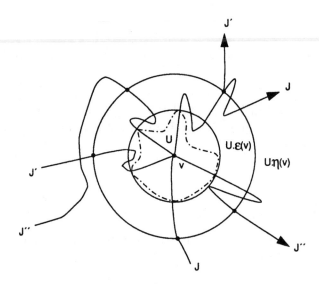

Figure 2.5: The neighborhood U of Lemma 2.3.2.

See Figure 2.5 for an illustration. Let $\alpha_1, \ldots, \alpha_k$ denote the *different* subarcs of bisecting curves $J(p,q)$ that connect v with one of the two points in $J(p,q) \cap \partial U$, and let α_{0i} denote α_i without its endpoints, where $1 \leq i \leq k$. Clearly,

$$V(S) \cap U \subseteq \{v\} \cup \bigcup_{i=1}^{k} \alpha_{0i}$$

holds, due to **) and Lemma 2.2.1, 3). By Lemma 2.3.2, each α_{0i} fulfills the condition of Lemma 2.2.2 and must therefore be entirely contained in one Voronoi region. Assume that $\alpha_{0i} \subset R(p, S)$ and that $\alpha_{0i} \cap V(S) \neq \emptyset$. Then α_{0i} contains a point $w \in R(p, S) \cap \overline{R(q, S)} \subseteq J(p, q)$, for some point $q \in S$, and must therefore be contained in $J(p, q)$. But $\alpha_{0i} \subset R(p, S) \cap J(p, q)$ implies $\alpha_{0i} \subset V(S)$, due to Lemma 2.2.1, 3). *Thus, each α_{0i} is either contained in $V(S)$ or disjoint from it* .

Let $\beta_{01}, \ldots, \beta_{0l}$ denote those α_{0i} contained in $V(S)$, and let $\beta_i := \beta_{0i} \cup \{v\}$ if $\beta_i \subset R(p_\mu, S)$ (see the third property in $*$)), $\beta_i := \beta_{0i}$, otherwise. Then

$$V(S) \cap U = \bigcup_{i=1}^{l} \beta_i.$$

The closure of each β_i contains a point w_i in ∂U. These points are pairwise different. Because ∂U is a simple closed curve (Lemma 2.3.2), a cyclical order is defined among the w_i by the counterclockwise orientation of ∂U. If $U' \subset U$ is a smaller neighborhood of v fulfilling Lemma 2.3.2 then each β_i is intersected exactly once by $\partial U'$, and the counterclockwise order of these intersections along $\partial U'$ corresponds to the order among the w_i, because the curve segments β_i do not cross. Thus, a *cyclical order among the β_i at v* is induced that does not depend on U. In the following, we assume that the β_i are indexed in such a way that $(\beta_1, \beta_2, \ldots, \beta_l)$ is their cyclical order.

The domain U is split by the β_i into l subdomains. Due to Corollary 2.2.3, each of these domains is entirely contained in one Voronoi region. Let $R(p_i, S)$ be the region that contains the domain bounded by β_i, β_{i+1}, and by a segment of ∂U, where indices must be read mod l. Furthermore, let $R(q_i, S)$ be the region containing β_i, see Figure 2.6.

Lemma 2.3.3   *1. $l \geq 2$.*

2. $p_i \neq p_{i+1}$ for $i = 1, \ldots, l$.

Proof: 1) If $l = 0$ then $V(S) \cap U = \{v\}$, hence $U - \{v\} \subseteq R(p_1, S)$. The point v must belong to a different region, hence $p_1 \neq p_\mu$ (see $*$)). Since $R(p_\mu, S)$ is path-connected, due to the definition of an admissible system, it follows that $R(p_\mu, S) = \{v\}$ has no interior, contradicting Definition 2.1.2, A). Hence, $l \geq 1$. The proof of 2) shows that l must be at least 2.

2) Suppose there were a point $w \in \beta_i$ such that $U_\varrho(w) - \beta_i \subset R(p_i, S)$ holds for small enough ϱ. Then $p_i \neq q_i$ (the region containing β_i) since $w \in V(S)$, hence $\beta_i \subset J(p_i, q_i)$. Thus, there are points of (q_i, p_i) in $U_\varrho(w)$, and these do neither belong to β_i nor to $R(p_i, S)$, a contradiction!   □

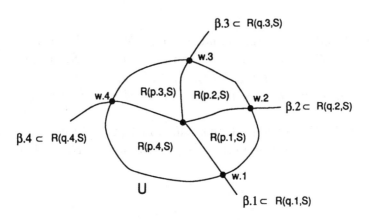

Figure 2.6: Notations.

For each β_i two cases may arise.

Case 1 $q_i \in \{p_{i-1}, p_i\}$.
In this case β_i belongs to the common boundary of the neighboring Voronoi regions $R(p_{i-1}, S)$ and $R(p_i, S)$. If $p_i < p_{i-1}$ then $\beta_i \subset R(p_i, S)$, otherwise $\beta_i \subset R(p_{i-1}, S)$. Clearly, $\beta_i \subset J(p_{i-1}, p_i)$.

Case 2 $q_i \notin \{p_{i-1}, p_i\}$.
Here we have $\beta_i \subset \partial R(p_{i-1}, S) \cap \partial R(p_i, S)$, too, but these regions are not neighbors along β_i, because between them runs $R(q_i, S)$. The common borderline of $R(p_{i-1}, S)$ and $R(q_i, S)$, and the common borderline of $R(q_i, S)$ and $R(p_i, S)$, are both lying over β_i. Clearly, $q_i < \min\{p_{i-1}, p_i\}$ and $\beta_i \subset J(p_{i-1}, q_i) \cap J(q_i, p_i) \cap J(p_{i-1}, p_i)$.

Definition 2.3.4 A triplet (β, p, q) is called a *borderline w.r.t.* S iff $\beta \subset R(p, S) \cap \overline{R(q, S)}$ is connected and contains at least two points. The borderline (β, p, q) is said to *lie over* β. A borderline of type (β, p, q) or (β, q, p) is often referred to as a $\{p, q\}$- or as a *p-borderline*, and denoted by $(\beta, \{p, q\})$.

If (β, p, q) is a borderline then $\beta \subset J(p, q)$ and $p < q$. The set $V(S)$ is the union of all β that give rise to borderlines with respect to S. At most two borderlines can lie over the same curve segment. In the above Case 2, β_i induces two borderlines, (β_i, q_i, p_{i-1}) and (β_i, q_i, p_i).

The cyclical order among the curve segments β_j can be extended to borderlines in a natural way : In Case 2 the borderline (β_i, q_i, p_{i-1}) comes before (β_i, q_i, p_i), corresponding to the order the Voronoi regions are met when marching around

∂U counterclockwise. These intersections are *intervals of ∂U of five possible types*: $[w, w]$, $[w_1, w_2]$, $[w_1, w_2)$, $(w_1, w_2]$, and (w_1, w_2), where $w_1 < w_2$ with respect to the cyclical order. Each occurence of a one-point interval $[w_i, w_i]$ corresponds to a curve segment β_i Case 2 applies to; see Figure 2.8. We use $< w_1, w_2 >$ to denote an interval of any of these five types.

Summarizing we obtain

Theorem 2.3.5 *For each point $v \in V(S)$ there exist arbitrarily small neighborhoods U having the following properties. Let $R(p_1, S)$, $R(p_2, S)$, ..., $R(p_h, S)$ be the sequence of Voronoi regions traversed on a counterclockwise march around the boundary of U, and let $I_1, I_2, \ldots, I_h$ denote the corresponding intervals of ∂U, where $I_j =< w_j, w_{j+1} >\subset R(p_j, S)$ for $1 \leq j \leq h$. Where I_{j-1} ends and I_j begins, a borderline with respect to S is crossed that lies over a curve segment β_j connecting v to w_j. Each one-point interval I_j gives rise to two borderlines over the same curve segment $\beta_j = \beta_{j+1}$; but different β_i have at most the point v in common. $V(S) \cap U$ is the union of the curve segments β_j. Each β_j is contained in the Voronoi region of $\min\{p_{j-1}, p_j\}$. The open "piece of pie" bordered by β_j, β_{j+1}, and by I_j, if not empty, belongs to $R(p_j, S)$. We always have $p_{j-1} \neq p_j$, and $p_{j-1} \neq p_{j+1}$ if I_j is a single point. The point v belongs to the region of $p_\mu := \min\{p_1, \ldots, p_h\}$, and this is the only region that can be encountered more than once on the march around ∂U.*

    Proof: Only the last assertion remains to be proven. Assume $p_i = p_j > p_\mu$. Then I_i and I_j are separated on ∂U by intervals $I_a \subset R(p_a, S)$, $I_b \subset R(p_b, S)$ such that $i < a < j < b$ and $p_i \notin \{p_a, p_b\}$. Since $v \notin R(p_i, S)$, the two pieces, T_i and T_j, of $R(p_i, S)$ bordered by I_i and I_j are not connected via v. Hence, they can be connected by an arc $\alpha \subset R(p_i, S)$ that avoids v. The arc α can be continued to a closed curve in $\overline{R(p_i, S)}$ that encircles points of $R(p_a, S)$, or of $R(p_b, S)$, see Figure 2.7. But this contradicts Lemma 2.2.4 ! $\Box$

Note that the number h and the cyclical sequence of the p_j, together with the corresponding interval types, do not depend on the neighborhood, U, but on v alone.

Definition 2.3.6 If the above theorem holds for a neighborhood U of a point v of $V(S)$ then U is called an *admissible neighborhood* of v w.r.t. S.

Figure 2.8 gives an example of a possible neighborhood of a point $v \in V(S)$. Here the pieces marked with an encircled p_i belong to $R(p_i, S)$, and we have $p_\mu = p_4 = p_7 = p_9$.

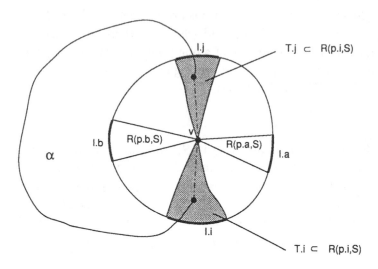

Figure 2.7: No region is represented twice, except the one containing v.

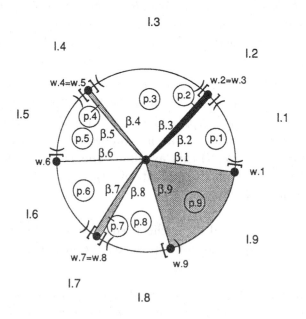

Figure 2.8: Nine borderlines radiating from v; $p_4 = p_7 = p_9 = p_\mu = \min\{p_1, \ldots, p_9\}$.

2.4   Augmented curve systems

Due to Remark 2.2.5, $V(S)$ contains at least one unbounded segment of a bisecting curve $J(p,q)$, if $|S| \geq 2$. To study the behaviour of such segments it is useful to compactify the plane by adding the "point at infinity". This is usually achieved by applying the stereographic projection, SP, that establishes a homeomorphism between the plane and the surface of the sphere less its north pole which now serves as the infinite point $v = \infty$. The image, $SP(J)$, of a bisecting curve J can be continued to a simple closed curve that passes ∞.

Because of the finiteness assumption 1) of Definition 2.1.2 there exist admissible neighborhoods of $v = \infty$, too, and all of Theorem 2.3.5 holds true, except for the last sentence. In fact, the point ∞ does not belong to any Voronoi region, and it can happen that several Voronoi regions are encountered more than once on a march around $v = \infty$ (regions bounded by parallel lines, for example). In order to avoid this anomaly, we shall *not* add the infinite point to $V(S)$. Instead, given an admissible system of bisecting curves w.r.t. S, we will fix an admissible neighborhood, U_∞, of $v = \infty$ on the sphere, and simply cut off the part of $SP(V(S))$ that lies inside U_∞. In the plane, this means to disregard all parts of $V(S)$ that lie in the outer domain of the simple closed curve $\Gamma := SP^{-1}(\partial U_\infty)$; see Figure 2.9.

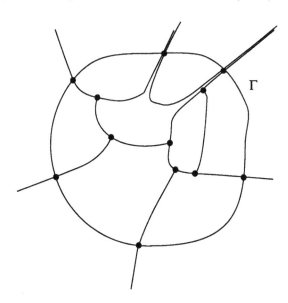

Figure 2.9: $V(S) \cap I(\Gamma)$.

By the definition of admissible neighborhoods, each curve segment, having reached Γ from its inner domain, will not intersect other segments nor be separated from one it is coincident with, as it tends to infinity; thus, no information gets lost by disregarding these segments. The cyclical order of the unbounded segments "at infinity" is captured by the order the curve Γ is intersected.

This approach fits in well with the notion of abstract Voronoi diagrams; we just have to assume that an additional point, ∞, is added to S, where $J(\infty, p) = \Gamma$ holds for all $p \in S$.

Definition 2.4.1 A system $(S, \mathcal{J})$ is called an *augmented system of bisecting curves* iff the following conditions are fulfilled.

1. $\infty \in S$.

2. $J(p, \infty) = J(\infty, p) = \Gamma$, for all finite $p \in S$, where Γ is the inverse image under stereographic projection of the boundary of an admissible neighborhood of ∞ w.r.t. $S - \{\infty\}$ in the sense of Definition 2.3.6.

3. $(S - \{\infty\}, \mathcal{J} - \{\Gamma\})$ is admissible in the sense of Definition 2.1.2.

Of course, $D(p, \infty)$ is defined to be the inner domain of Γ, and $p < \infty$ holds for finite $p \in S$. Each augmented system fulfills properties 1 and 2, *A)* and *B)*, of Definition 2.1.2. However, an augmented curve system contains one closed curve, namely, the augmenting curve Γ. Consequently, Lemma 2.2.4 holds only for those Voronoi regions $R(p, S)$ where $p \neq \infty$, because $R(\infty, S)$ is *not* simply-connected. Note that only three neighborhood types are possible for the points of Γ, see Figure 2.11.

For the rest of this chapter we will consider augmented systems $(S, \mathcal{J})$.

Finally, we show that almost all points of $V(S)$ have very simple neighborhoods.

Lemma 2.4.2 *For all but finitely many points of $V(S)$ the admissible neighborhoods are of one of the two simple types shown in Figure 2.10.*

Proof: Due to the finiteness assumption (Definition 2.1.2, 1)), only finitely many points of $V(S)$ are endpoints of a connected component of an intersection $J(p, q) \cap J(r, s)$, where p, q, r, $s \in S$. Let v belong to the rest. Then all bisecting curves that contain v must coincide in a small admissible neighborhood of v. Hence, there can be only two curve segments radiating from v. Besides the configurations shown in Figure 2.10 two more types exist having two emanating

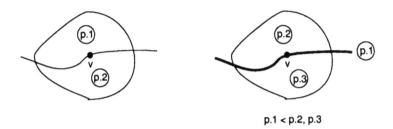

Figure 2.10: Simple neighborhoods.

segments, see Figure 2.12. Of these, the first one is impossible because β_1 cannot—like β_2—be contained in $J(p_\mu, p_1) \cap J(p_\mu, p_2) \subset R(p_\mu, \{p_\mu, p_1, p_2\})$. In the second picture, the point v belongs to $J(p_\mu, p_1) \subset R(p_\mu, p_1)$, and so must β_1, contradicting $\beta_1 \subset R(p_1, \{p_1, p_2, p_3, p_\mu\})$.   □

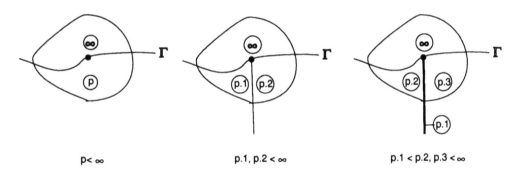

Figure 2.11: Neighborhoods of points of Γ.

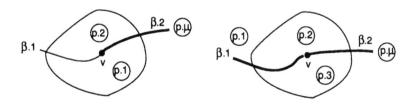

Figure 2.12: Not simple neighborhoods.

2.5   The shape of the Voronoi regions

The purpose of this section is in proving that a region of an abstract Voronoi diagram is bordered by a closed curve that results from squeezing together a simple closed curve in finitely many segments. A short tour through this section starts with the Definitions 2.5.1 and 2.5.2, and continues with Theorem 2.5.5.

As in Theorem 2.3.5, let $v \in V(S)$, $S' = \{p \in S; v \in \overline{R(p, S)}\}$, and $p_\mu = \min S'$. Furthermore, let

$$b_j := (\beta_j, \{p_{j-1}, p_j\}), \ 1 \leq j \leq h,$$

denote the borderlines radiating from v in an admissible neighborhood, U, of v, in counterclockwise order. Recall that for two consecutive borderlines, b_j and b_{j+1}, I_j denotes the interval of ∂U from the point of intersection of b_j with ∂U to the one of b_{j+1}.

Definition 2.5.1 A tuple (v, B) is called a *point induced by v w.r.t. S* iff $B = \{b_k, b_{k+1}, \ldots, b_{k+l}\}$ is a set of consecutive borderlines such that the intervals I_{k-1} and I_{k+l} belong to $R(p_\mu, S)$ but none of the intervals between them does.

Here I_{k-1} is the interval on ∂U terminated by b_k, and I_{k+l} is the one starting behind b_{k+l}; indices must be read mod h. The point v induces as many points as there are "pieces of pie" in U that belong to $R(p_\mu, S)$; these pieces *separate* the induced points (formally, we should have used *germs* (see [22], App.2) of borderlines to make the above definition independent of the neighborhood U, but our sloppyness will do no harm).

Figure 2.13 shows the three points induced by the point displayed in Figure 2.8. We have

$$\begin{aligned}
B_1 &= \{(\beta_8, p_\mu, p_8), (\beta_9, p_\mu, p_8)\} \\
B_2 &= \{(\beta_1, p_\mu, p_1), (\beta_2, p_2, p_1), (\beta_3, p_2, p_3), (\beta_4, p_\mu, p_3)\} \\
B_3 &= \{(\beta_5, p_\mu, p_5), (\beta_6, p_6, p_5), (\beta_7, p_\mu, p_6)\}
\end{aligned}$$

The following definition generalizes the incidence relation "v lies on β" to induced points and borderlines.

Definition 2.5.2 1. A point (v, B) *lies on* a borderline (β, p, q) iff there exists (β', p, q) in B such that $\beta' \subseteq \beta$ holds (in a small enough neighborhood of v).
2. If, in addition, there exists (β'', p, q) in B such that $\beta'' \subset \beta$ and $\beta' \cap \beta'' = \{v\}$ then (β, p, q) is said to *pass* the point (v, B).

Plain incidence is related to the relation just defined as follows.

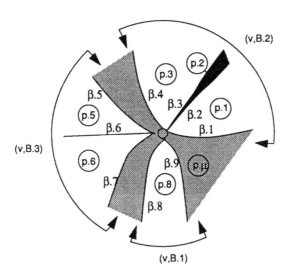

Figure 2.13: Three points induced by the point v of Figure 2.8 ; $p_\mu = p_4 = p_7 = p_9$.

Lemma 2.5.3 *Let (β, p, q) be a maximal borderline, and let $v \in \overline{\beta}$. Then there is precisely one point (v, B) induced by v that lies on (β, p, q), and for this point the following assertions are equivalent.*

1. *v is not an endpoint of β.*

2. *(β, p, q) passes (v, B).*

3. *$|B| = 2$.*

Proof: If v is a (possibly not included) endpoint of β then (β, p, q) belongs to exactly one point induced by v. If β doesn't end at v then it gives rise to two borderlines, $b' = (\beta', p, q)$ and $b'' = (\beta'', p, q)$, radiating from v. Since $p < q$ the region $R(q, S)$ is encountered only once on a march around v, due to Theorem 2.3.5; this piece must be bordered by b' and b''. Furthermore, $p = p_\mu = \min S'$ must hold. Thus, v induces the point (v, B), where $B = \{b', b''\}$. Since $p = p_\mu$ we have $v \in \beta' \cap \beta''$, hence (β, p, q) passes (v, B), see the piece of $R(p_8, S)$ in Figure 2.13. Conversely, if the set B of an arbitrary induced node (v, B) consists of two elements only, then these must be of the form (β', p_μ, q), (β'', p_μ, q), and the maximal (p_μ, q)-borderline containing β' or β'' contains $\beta' \cup \{v\} \cup \beta''$ and passes (v, B). □

Next, we turn to a close examination of the shape of the Voronoi regions. From Theorem 2.3.5 we know all possible neighborhood types a point on a region

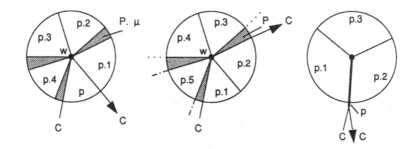

Figure 2.14: Tracing the p-border.

boundary can have, see also Figure 2.11. Furthermore, Lemma 2.4.2 ensures that most of them are simple. Now we put together the local information.

Since the underlying curve system is augmented, exactly one of the Voronoi regions is unbounded: $R(\infty, S)$, the outer domain of the simple closed curve Γ (cf. 2.4). The other Voronoi regions form a partition of $I(\Gamma) \cup \Gamma$, where $I(\Gamma)$ denotes the inner domain of Γ. Hence, they are bounded. Let $R(p, S)$ be one of the *bounded* regions, and let $v \in \partial R(p, S)$ be a point whose neighborhood is simple. If two p-borderlines are induced by the curve segment containing v (the second case depicted in Figure 2.10, where $p_1 = p$) then we fix one of them. Now we *trace* the continuation of this p-borderline in any direction as follows. Whenever a point w is reached whose neighborhood is not simple we follow the p-borderline leaving w that belongs to the same point induced by v as the one that has lead us to w, see Figure 2.14. Because there are only finitely many such points w, and since the borderlines are bounded, we will eventually arrive at the same borderline containing v we have started from. Until then, some points w may have been visited several times, but each induced point has been encountered at most once. Thus, we have traced a *closed curve, C,* that has at most finitely many self-intersections where different segments touch, but no crossings.

As any closed curve, C dissects the plane into disjoint domains exactly one of which, D_∞, is unbounded. Let $I(C)$ denote the union of the bounded domains. Since $C \subset \overline{R(p, S)}$, Lemma 2.2.4 implies $I(C) \subset R(p, S)$. Hence, those pieces of the neighborhoods shown in Figure 2.14 that do not belong to $R(p, S)$ are included in D_∞.

A point v can be a multiple point of the curve C only if at least two points are induced by v. In this case, two p-borderlines are incident to each induced node, each pair being a possible candidate for a subarc of C, see the second drawing of Figure 2.14.

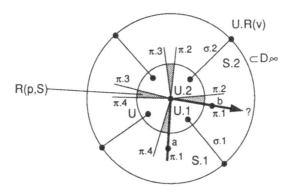

Figure 2.15: A wheel.

Lemma 2.5.4 *If $v \in C$ then all the p-borderline pairs arising from the points induced by v are visited by C in succession, corresponding to their cyclical order around v.*

Proof: Assume that at least two points are induced by v. Let (v, B_1), (v, B_2), $\ldots$, (v, B_m) denote the points induced by v, in counterclockwise order. The p-borderline pair π_i in B_i cuts a subdomain, U_i, off the neighborhood U of v that is contained in D_∞, because it doesn't belong to $R(p, S)$; see Figure 2.15. Let R be large enough such that $\overline{U}$ is contained in $U_R(v)$, and that $\partial U_R(v) \subset D_\infty$. For each $i \leq m$ let $\sigma_i \subset D_\infty$ be an arc joining an arbitrary point of U_i with $\partial U_R(v)$ such that $\sigma_i \cap \sigma_j = \emptyset$ if $i \neq j$. This arrangement looks like a wheel, the σ_i being the spokes connecting the nave, U, to the rim, $\partial U_R(v)$. The space between rim and nave, $U_R(v) - \overline{U}$, is dissected into domains $S_1, S_2, \ldots, S_m$ by the spokes. Assume that the p-borderline pair π_1 belongs to C. Then C runs from a point $a \in S_1$ to a point $b \in S_2$. But C ist a closed curve, so it has to return to a without intersecting a spoke or the rim, since these are part of D_∞. Inside U, only the p-borderline pairs are allowed for C, and each of them can be used at most once. Thus, C cannot but follow the successive gateways $\pi_2, \pi_3, \ldots, \pi_m$ in order to return to b, see Figure 2.16. $\qquad\square$

Theorem 2.5.5 *For each $p \in S$ is the boundary of $R(p, S)$ a closed curve, consisting of a sequence $\alpha_1, \ldots, \alpha_k$ of arcs $\alpha_j \subset J(p, p_j)$. Without its endpoints, each α_j induces a p-borderline $(\beta_j, \{p, p_j\})$. The finitely many self-intersections the curve $\partial R(p, S)$ can have arise from arcs α_i, α_j that touch; then $p_i \neq p_j$ and $p < p_i, p_j$. If p is finite then the interior of $R(p, S)$ is the union of the finitely many inner domains of $\partial R(p, S)$.*

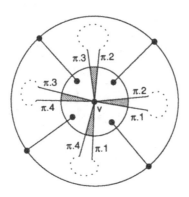

Figure 2.16: The course of C.

Figure 2.17: Impossible decompositions of a region boundary.

Proof: If $p = \infty$ then $\partial R(p, S) = \Gamma$, and the assertions are clear. Let $p \neq \infty$. We show that the curve C constructed above is the full boundary of $R(p, S)$. If there were a p-borderline not visited by C one could construct a second closed curve, C' that, as a consequence of Lemma 2.5.4, would be disjoint from C. Since each point of C' belongs to the closure of a Voronoi region different from p, it cannot be contained in one of the bounded domains in the complement of C, thereby ruling out the first case depicted in Figure 2.17. But the second case is also impossible because $R(p, S)$ is path-connected. Therefore, $\partial R(p, S) = C$, and the other assertions follow.   □

Figure 3.30 shows the possible shape of a Voronoi region. Points of any two, D_a and D_b, of the inner domains can be connected by an arc in $R(p, S)$. Such an arc visits *cut-points* of $R(p, S)$, arising from self-intersections of $\partial R(p, S)$, whose removal would disconnect the Voronoi region.

We now start to *thicken* these thin parts of the regions conceptually by separating coincident borderlines and induced points. However, this is only done in order to capture the proper graph structure of the Voronoi diagram; we are *not* going to actually change the Voronoi regions.

2.6 The graph structure of abstract Voronoi diagrams

Let us assume that the set S contains at least two finite points besides ∞, in order to avoid trivial cases.

Definition 2.6.1 Let $\widehat{V}(S)$ denote the graph with vertex set

$$\mathcal{V} := \{(v, B) \text{ induced by } V(S); |B| \geq 3\}$$

and edge set

$$\mathcal{E} := \left\{ \begin{array}{c} (\nu_1, \nu_2) \in \mathcal{V}^2; \text{ there is a borderline } b \text{ w.r.t. } S \text{ such that} \\ \nu_1, \nu_2 \text{ lie on } b \end{array} \right\}$$

Theorem 2.6.2 $\widehat{V}(S)$ *is a planar graph each of whose vertices is of degree at least* 3. $\widehat{V}(S)$ *has* $|S|$ *faces, and* $O(|S|)$ *edges and vertices.* $V(S)$ *results from an embedding of* $\widehat{V}(S)$ *by means of a deformation that is limit of admissible deformations.*

An *embedding* of a graph is a mapping that sends vertices to different points in the plane, and edges to curves that connect the mapped images of their incident vertices and do not intersect otherwise. A deformation of an embedding of a planar graph is *admissible* if it is continuous and an embedding at each stage.

Proof: Being bounded, each maximal borderline of two bounded Voronoi regions has vertices of $\widehat{V}(S)$ as endpoints, due to Lemma 2.5.3. According to Remark 2.2.5, at least one vertex is incident with Γ, the boundary of $R(\infty, S)$. Thus, each maximal borderline gives rise to an edge of $\widehat{V}(S)$. Conversely, each edge stems from a maximal borderline, because a borderline cannot *pass through* a vertex (Lemma 2.5.3). To define an embedding of $\widehat{V}(S)$ in the plane, let v be one of the finitely many points whose neighborhood is not simple (see Figure 2.10 and Lemma 2.4.2), and let $U_\varepsilon(v)$ be contained in an admissible neighborhood, U, of v.

If two or more points are induced by v then these are mapped to different points of $\partial U_\varepsilon(v)$, preserving the cyclical order among them. Figure 2.18 shows

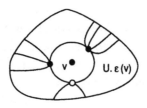

Figure 2.18: The mapped images of the points induced by v of Figure 2.13.

what happens to the point v of Figure 2.13; here the two vertices induced are marked with filled dots, the third point with an empty one. If (v, B) is the only vertex induced by v then it is mapped onto v. The mapped images of the points induced by v are now connected to the boundary of U, using separate arcs for different borderline segment radiating from v, see Figure 2.18. The finitely many "units" thus obtained can easily be "wired"; no crossing can occur outside the units.

This gives us an embedding, i, of $\widehat{V}(S)$ in the plane. Clearly, i can be re-deformed into a mapping j that maps $\widehat{V}(S)$ onto $V(S)$ in the way stated in the Theorem. The resulting map, $i(\widehat{V}(S))$, has $n = |S|$ faces, one to each Voronoi region, because the connectivity of the regions is preserved and no two regions have united. By definition, at least 3 edges are incident with each vertex of $\widehat{V}(S)$. Now the assertion follows as in the proof of Lemma 1.1.1.   □

Definition 2.6.3 The abstract Voronoi diagram $V(S)$ is called *regular* iff no point of $V(S)$ induces more than one point, that is iff the boundary of each region is a simple closed curve. In this case, $i(\widehat{V}(S)) = V(S)$. The map i is called a *natural embedding* of $\widehat{V}(S)$.

Figure 2.19 shows how $\widehat{V}(S)$, $i(\widehat{V}(S))$, and $V(S)$ are related in general.

2.7   Characterizing Voronoi diagrams

This section is entirely independent of the other chapters.

Given a partition, V, of the plane into finitely many regions, it is natural to ask if V is a Voronoi diagram out of a given class. It has been studied by Ash and Bolker how to recognize Euclidean Voronoi diagrams [5] and diagrams based on more general distance functions of "power"-type, see [4] and [6].

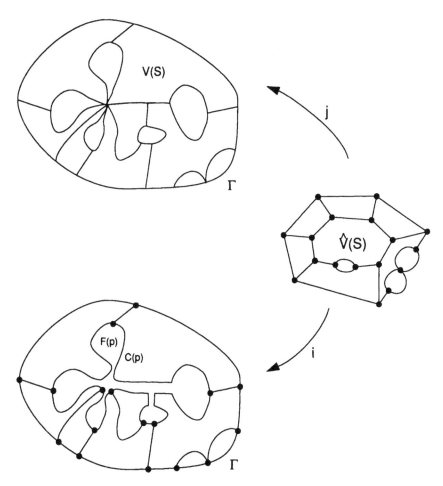

Figure 2.19: A Voronoi diagram, and the embedding of the graph induced.

Even in the Euclidean case this recognition problem is non-trivial. For V to be a Euclidean Voronoi diagram, each region must be a (possibly unbounded) convex polygon (i.e., the intersection of finitely many halfplanes). Assume that the point v belongs to the boundary of $d \geq 3$ different regions. Let $\vartheta_1, \vartheta_2, \ldots, \vartheta_d$ denote the consecutive angles between the d line segments $\beta_1, \ldots, \beta_d$ radiating from v, see Figure 2.20. If V is a Voronoi diagram then the region R_i bordered by β_i and β_{i+1} is the Voronoi region of a point p_i; here and in the following, indices must be read mod d. Let α_i denote the angle between β_i and the ray from v to p_i. Clearly, $\alpha_i > 0$ for $i = 1, \ldots, d$.

Each line segment β_{i+1} is part of the perpendicular bisector of p_i and p_{i+1}, therefore

$$\vartheta_i = \alpha_i + \alpha_{i+1} \quad \text{for} \quad i = 1, \ldots, d.$$

Now assume that d *is odd*. Then, by substituting the above equalities,

$$\begin{aligned}
\vartheta_1 - \vartheta_2 + \vartheta_3 - \ldots - \vartheta_{d-1} + \vartheta_d &= \alpha_1 + \alpha_2 - (\alpha_2 + \alpha_3) + (\alpha_3 + \alpha_4) \\
&\quad - \ldots - (\alpha_{d-1} + \alpha_d) + (\alpha_d + \alpha_1) \\
&= 2\alpha_1
\end{aligned}$$

and similary

$$(*) \qquad \alpha_i = \frac{1}{2} \sum_{j=0}^{d-1} (-1)^j \vartheta_{i+j} \quad \text{for} \quad i = 1, \ldots, d.$$

Thus, for V to be a Voronoi diagram it is *necessary* that all the alternating sums in $(*)$ have positive values! Clearly, these are *local* conditions for vertex v; if they are fulfilled then the direction of p_i, as seen from v, is uniquely determined: p_i must lie on the ray $\rho(v, R_i)$ that radiates from v at an angle of α_i with respect to β_i. This gives rise to an obvious *global* necessity condition. Namely, if $v_1, \ldots, v_m$ are the vertices of region R, then the rays $\rho(v_1, R), \ldots, \rho(v_m, R)$ must have a point in common. In many cases, these conditions are sufficient, too.

Theorem 2.7.1 *(Ash/Bolker, 1985) Let V be a partition of the plane into finitely many convex polygons, that contains at least one vertex. Assume that each vertex of V is of odd degreee, and that one can march around each vertex v in such a way that all the unbounded line segments emanating from v are met first. Then the following assertions are equivalent.*

1. *V is a Euclidean Voronoi diagram.*

2. *For each vertex of V all the alternating sums $(*)$ are positive, and for each region R of V the rays of the adjacent vertices, $\rho(v_1, R), \ldots, \rho(v_m, R)$, have a point in common.*

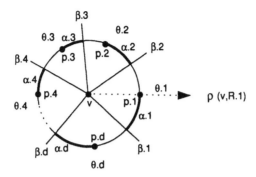

Figure 2.20: The neighborhood of an Euclidean Voronoi diagram vertex.

Things become more involved if vertices of even degree are considered, because here the angles α_i are no longer uniquely determined by the ϑ_i; the reader is referred to the above mentioned work.

Now we turn to the class of abstract Voronoi diagrams. This class being more general, the recognition problem turns out to be much simpler. Recall that a graph is called *biconnected* iff it is connected and contains no *cut-vertex* whose removal would disconnect the graph.

Lemma 2.7.2 *Let $V(S)$ be an abstract Voronoi diagram based on an augmented system of curves. Then $\widehat{V}(S)$ is biconnected.*

Proof: If $i(\widehat{V}(S))$ were not connected it would contain a connected component, Z, that is not connected to Γ, the boundary of the infinite face. Thus, there exists a simple closed curve C containing Z in its interior domain, $I(C)$, such that C is fully contained in a bounded face F. By definition of $\widehat{V}(S)$, the component Z cannot consist of an isolated vertex. Let e be an edge of Z, and let w be a point of e; then each neighborhood of w contains elements of at least two different faces, due to Lemma 2.3.3. If $F' \neq F$ and $F' \cap I(C) \neq \emptyset$ then face F' is encircled by $C \subset F$, a contradiction to Lemma 2.2.4.

Now suppose that removing a vertex $\hat{v}$ disconnects $i(\widehat{V}(S))$. Let E denote the set of edges formerly incident to $\hat{v}$. First, assume that $\hat{v}$ does not belong to Γ. By assumption, there are edges in E that are not connected to Γ, if $\hat{v}$ is removed. Let $e_1, \ldots, e_r$ be a maximal sequence of successive edges of this type, as they appear on a march around $\hat{v}$ (Figure 2.21). The part of $i(\widehat{V}(S))$ that is connected to an edge out of $e_1, \ldots, e_r$ can be encircled by a simple closed curve, C, that is contained in $F \cup \{\hat{v}\}$, for some bounded face F. One concludes as above that a face $F' \neq F$ must be encircled by C; again, this contradicts Lemma 2.2.4. If $\hat{v}$ belongs to Γ

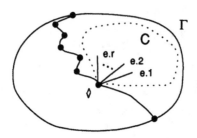

Figure 2.21: No cut-vertex is contained in $i(\widehat{V}(S))$.

then the same argumentation can be applied to those incident edges that are not part of Γ, cf. Figure 2.11.   □

For the following, let Γ be a simple closed curve. An embedded planar graph M is called a Γ-*map* iff M has at least 3 faces, one of them being the closure of the outer domain of Γ. Let $I(\Gamma)$ denote the inner domain. Finally, recall that the endpoints of an arc are different, by definition.

Theorem 2.7.3 *For each Γ-map M the following assertions are equivalent.*

1. *There exists an augmented system $(S, \mathcal{J})$ with $\Gamma \in \mathcal{J}$ such that $V(S)$ is regular and equal to M.*

2. *M is biconnected. Each vertex of M is of degree ≥ 3; the vertices on Γ are of degree 3.*

3. *M can be constructed by repeated insertions of arcs each of which bisects a face obtained in a previous step, starting with $\overline{I(\Gamma)}$. At most one arc is attached to each point of Γ.*

Proof: 2) follows from 1) by Lemma 2.7.2 and Theorem 2.6.2; see also Figure 2.11.

2) $\Longrightarrow$ 3): By induction on the number of edges. It follows from [10], Chap. I, Theorem 3.7, that there exists an edge in M that can be removed without destroying the biconnectedness. However, we need that such an edge can be found which is not part of Γ; thus, we shall give a direct proof. It is sufficient to show the following (cf. [10], Chap. I, Corollary 3.2).

Lemma 2.7.4 *Let M be a planar map with 3 faces or more, all of whose vertices are of degree at least 3. Suppose that M is biconnected. Then there exists an edge*

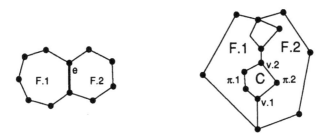

Figure 2.22: Looking for a removable edge.

e bordering two bounded faces of M such that the endpoints of e can be connected by two (internally) vertex-disjoint paths in M that do not contain e.

Proof: By assumption, M has at least two bounded faces, besides the unbounded one. Since M is biconnected there are no self-loops in M, and each edge borders two different faces (otherwise, the removal of a vertex incident with such an edge would disconnect the graph). The boundary of each face is a simple edge cycle. Moreover, there must be two bounded faces, F_1 and F_2, that have an edge in common. If this edge, e, is all of $F_1 \cap F_2$ then $\partial F_1 - e$ and $\partial F_2 - e$ are the desired vertex-disjoint paths that join the endpoints of e, see the first picture of Figure 2.22.

If $F_1 \cap F_2$ consists of two or more components (edges and vertices), let C denote one of the simple cycles consisting of (internally) vertex-disjoint paths $\pi_i \subset \partial F_i, i = 1, 2$, that connect two successive components of $F_1 \cap F_2$ and encircles one or more faces different from F_1 and F_2; see the second drawing of Figure 2.22. If π_1 is a single edge then π_2 and $\partial F_1 - \pi_1$ are internally vertex-disjoint paths joining the endpoints of π_1. The same holds for π_2. If both, π_1 and π_2, consist of two edges or more let M' denote the graph obtained from M by removing all pieces outside C; if one of the endpoints, v_1 or v_2, of π_1 is of degree 3 this vertex is removed by glueing together the two remaining edges of C.

By induction, there is an edge e' in M' whose endpoints can be connected by vertex-disjoint paths in M' that do not contain e'. If e' is an edge of M the assertion follows. Otherwise, e' results from glueing together two edges, e_1 and e_2, of M that were formerly incident with—say—vertex v_1 of M, see Figure 2.23. One of the two paths, π', connecting the endpoints of e' must be (internally) vertex-disjoint from the edge cycle that circumscribes M'. Thus, the endpoints of edge e_1 can be connected by two disjoint paths in M, as depicted in Figure 2.23. $\square$

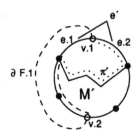

Figure 2.23: Endpoints of e_1 connected by two disjoint paths.

3) $\Longrightarrow$ 1): Let M be obtained from Γ by successive insertions of bisecting arcs, $\alpha_1, \ldots, \alpha_m$, where $m \geq 1$, since M has at least 3 faces. We define *labels* for the faces of M as follows. First, $I(\Gamma)$ is labelled by 1. If arc α_i, when inserted, bisects a face F of M whose label is p, then one of the two resulting subfaces of F inherits this label, whereas its buddy obtains the label $i+1$. Figure 2.24 shows an example and the corresponding partition tree, as produced using TreeTEX; see [12].

In what follows only *bounded* faces are considered. The internal nodes of the partition tree, T, correspond to the bisecting arcs, whereas the external nodes correspond to the faces of M. Two faces are *separated* by the arc assigned to the lowest common ancestor, a, of their external nodes, given Γ and the arcs along the path from the root of T to node a. We shall use this fact in defining an augmented curve system whose Voronoi diagram is M but, to this end, we first have to continue the bisecting arcs α_i to bisecting curves in such a way that the conditions of an admissible curve system (Definition 2.1.2) are fulfilled.

Each arc on the path to a face F of M in the partition tree is called an *F-arc*. The *F-side* of an F-arc, α, is the union of all faces of M that belong to the same subtree rooting at the node of α as F does. Clearly, F belongs to the F-side of each arc that contributes to the boundary of F. This notion generalizes to the larger faces that exist only during the insertion process. These are in one-to-one correspondence with the internal nodes of T: An internal node associated with arc α_i corresponds to the face bisected by α_i.

If z is a point of the boundary of F then there exists an arc γ, leading from z to Γ, that intersects an arbitrary F-arc in at most one point, and only on leaving its F-side. This can easily be seen by induction on m, the number of arcs inserted. In addition, one can assume that γ - without its endpoints - intersects no vertex of M and crosses each edge of M at most once; this can even be fulfilled for each Γ-map $\widetilde{M}$ resulting from M by adding finitely many additional edges that do not count as possible F-arcs. If one arc, γ, is given that has the above properties, we can find infinitely many "equivalent" arcs γ' close to γ, and on either side of γ,

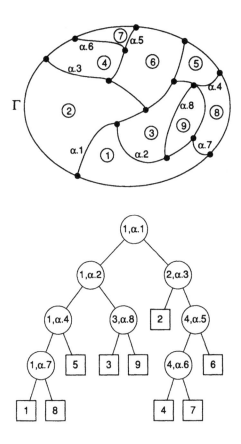

Figure 2.24: A Γ-map with corresponding partition tree.

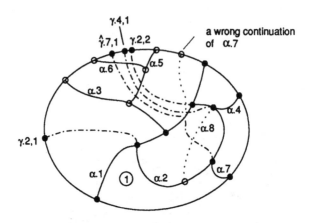

Figure 2.25: Extending the 1−arcs.

that have only the point z in common but show the same intersection behaviour (such arcs arise from different realizations of the same path in the planar dual of $\widetilde{M}$). Using these facts, one shows by induction on i that the arcs α_i can be continued as follows.

Lemma 2.7.5 *Each arc α_i can be continued to an arc A_i bisecting $\overline{I(\Gamma)}$ such that the following holds.*

- *Let F_j denote the face bisected by the insertion of α_j. Then each of the (possibly two) arcs of A_j that continue α_j intersects an ancestor arc, α_i, of α_j only on leaving the F_j-side of α_i. Moreover, we have $A_j - \alpha_j \cap A_i - \alpha_i = \emptyset$.*

- *$A_i \cap A_j$ consists of at most finitely many points, for arbitrary $i \neq j$.*

As a consequence, a face F_j cannot be trespassed by an extended F_j-arc A_i. For, the arc α_i does not intersect the interior of F_j, and the subarc(s) by which α_i is continued are not even allowed to enter the larger face, F_i, after starting from the endpoints of α_i in ∂F_i.

Figure 2.25 shows extensions of the 1-arcs α_1, α_2, α_4, and α_7 of Figure 2.24.

Now we can define an admissible curve system that corresponds to M. Let the arcs A_i of the lemma be continued to bisecting curves B_i by unbounded curve segments that are mutually disjoint. Let S_0 be the set of labels $1, 2, \ldots, m + 1$. For each pair of labels, p and q, let $J(p, q)$ denote the extension B_i of that arc α_i which separates the faces of M that are labelled with p and q. Finally, let $D(p, q)$ be the domain separated by $J(p, q)$ that contains the interior of the p-side of α_i.

By construction, for each $p \in S_0$

$$\overline{I(\Gamma)} \cap \overline{R(p, S_0)} = \text{the face of } M \text{ labelled with } p$$

holds. To prove claim 1) of the theorem we show by induction on m that *the Voronoi regions based on a non-empty subset S_0' of S_0 form a partition of the plane into path-connected sets with non-empty interiors.*

For $m = 1$ the assertion is obvious. Suppose that a new label, $m + 2$, has been added to S_0, corresponding to an arc α_{m+1} that bisects a face $F_p = \overline{I(\Gamma)} \cap \overline{R(p, S_0)}$ of M. By construction, we have

$$R(m + 2, q) = R(p, q)$$
$$R(q, m + 2) = R(q, p)$$

if $q \in S_0$, $q \neq p$, if the order among the sites is extended such that $m + 2 \prec q$ holds iff $p \prec q$. For each subset of $S_0 \cup \{m + 2\}$ not containing $m + 2$, the assertion follows directly by induction hypothesis. Let $S_0' \subseteq S_0$; if $p \notin S_0'$ then we have

$$R(q, S_0' \cup \{m + 2\}) = R(q, S_0' \cup \{p\})$$

if $q \in S_0'$, and

$$R(m + 2, S_0' \cup \{m + 2\}) = R(p, S_0' \cup \{p\}),$$

and again, the assertion follows by induction hypothesis. Assume $p \in S_0'$; then

$$
\begin{aligned}
R(q, S_0' \cup \{m + 2\}) &= R(q, S_0') \quad \text{if} \quad q \neq p, q \neq m + 2 \\
R(p, S_0' \cup \{m + 2\}) &= R(p, S_0') \cap R(p, m + 2) \\
R(m + 2, S_0' \cup \{m + 2\}) &= R(p, S_0') \cap R(m + 2, p)
\end{aligned}
$$

Due to the induction hypothesis, we have only to show that the latter two sets are path-connected, knowing that the contour of $R(p, S_0')$ consists of certain extensions of p-arcs, that is of arcs that are ancestors of α_{m+1} in the partition tree of $M \cup \{\alpha_{m+1}\}$. The arc α_{m+1} is included in $F_p \subseteq \overline{R(p, S_0)} \subseteq \overline{R(p, S_0')}$; it lies on the p-side of each arc that contributes to $\partial R(p, S_0')$. Thus, by the above lemma, each of the curve segments extending α_{m+1} to $J(p, m + 2)$ intersects $\partial R(p, S_0')$ in at most one point, namely on leaving this region. Therefore, $R(p, S_0')$ is partitioned into two path-connected subsets by $J(p, m + 2)$.

This completes the proof of the theorem. □

Here we have addressed only regular Voronoi diagrams. If deformations are considered that may cause edges to touch, an additional necessity condition arises: the relation "a cut-point of face p belongs to the closure of face q" must be acyclic.

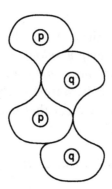

Figure 2.26: Not an abstract Voronoi diagram.

The deformed map shown in Figure 2.26, for example, cannot be obtained from an abstract Voronoi diagram.

Chapter 3

Computing abstract Voronoi diagrams

This chapter is concerned with the computation of abstract Voronoi diagrams. After a brief introduction to one of the standard ways of representing planar graphs, the divide-and-conquer approach is presented, as developed by Shamos and Hoey [56] for the Euclidean case.

For the sake of brevity, we shall no longer distinguish between $V(S)$ and the embedded graph $\widehat{V}(S)$, but simply consider $V(S)$ a possibly degenerate map. The main activity in constructing a Voronoi diagram by the divide-and-conquer technique consists in computing the *bisector* of two subsets, L and R, of the site set S, which consists of all those edges of $V(S)$ that are the common border of an L-face and an R-face. Under the assumption that this set of edges contains no cycle we first introduce a scheme of grouping these edges into chains (Section 3.3). Next, we turn to the problems in computing these bisecting chains. Here the non-degenerate case, where two bisecting curves can only cross transversally at a point, but not touch, is treated first (Section 3.4). The main difficulty is how to determine the endpoint of a bisecting chain segment correctly. In the Euclidean case, the endpoint of chain segment b is computed by scanning the contour of either region bisected by b; here performance depends on the order in which the prolongations of consecutive chain segments appear on a region contour. With curves instead of straight lines, this approach is to fail without additional assumptions. Surprisingly, the connectedness of the Voronoi regions turns out to be an assumption strong enough (Lemma 3.4.1.3, Theorem 3.4.1.5 and Theorem 3.4.1.6). Nevertheless, the standard clockwise/counterclockwise scan procedure has to undergo modifications. Finding the continuing chain segment, after the endpoint of its predecessor has been determined, is considered next.

Then we address the degenerate case, where bisecting curves are allowed to intersect in an arbitrary way. We show that one can separate the curves passing a given point v such that they do locally not intersect except at v, while preserving the local structure of each diagram $V(S')$, $S' \subseteq S$, without conflicts (Theorem 3.5.1.2). Having removed these degeneracies, the remaining task consists in determining the continuation of a bisecting chain from a multiple point of one or both of $V(L)$ and $V(R)$.

3.1   Representing the Voronoi diagram

Assume that an admissible curve system $(S_0, \mathcal{J}_0)$ is given (cf. Definition 2.1.2). Our task is to compute its Voronoi diagram, $V(S_0)$. To avoid unbounded curve segments we have chosen to encircle the interesting part of $V(S_0)$ by an simple closed curve, Γ, and to cut off what stands out (Section 2.4). It turned out that the resulting diagram, $V(S)$ results from the realization of a planar graph, $\widehat{V}(S)$, by "squeezing together" some faces (Theorems 2.5.5 and 2.6.2).

From now on, $V(S)$ will be referred to as a *(degenerate) planar map*, for the sake of simplicity. To avoid confusion, we will distinguish a *point v* from the *induced points*—in particular: from *vertices*—(v, B) of $V(S)$ (cf. Definition 2.5.1). Similary, we distinguish an *edge* of $V(S)$, which corresponds to a maximal borderline (β, p, q) (Definition 2.3.4), from the underlying curve $\beta \subset J(p, q)$. Each edge consists of induced points. The *faces* of the (degenerate) map $V(S)$ are the path connected sets

$$F_p = \overline{R(p, S)}.$$

Throughout this chapter, the augmented system $(S, \mathcal{J})$ is fixed, where $S = S_0 \cup \{\infty\}$ and $\mathcal{J} = \mathcal{J}_0 \cup \{\Gamma\}$. As before, we assume that a *fixed site*, p, has been chosen from the interior of each region $R(p, S)$. They will be identified with the elements of S. If the Voronoi diagram of a subset of S is considered, we suppose that the corresponding curves of J are used as separators. Finally, we let $n = |S_0|$.

In order to represent the Voronoi diagram we shall make use of a modified version of the *doubly-connected edge-list* (DCEL) introduced in [47]. This data structure is usually employed in storing a (non-degenerate) planar map M. To each edge e of M the DCEL of M contains one *edge record* that holds the following information. For each of the two vertices, v_1 and v_2, incident with e the edge record of e stores

- a pointer to the record of that edge e_i which is encountered first on a *counterclockwise* march around v_i, when starting from e.

- the name of that face of M which is bordered by e and by e_i.

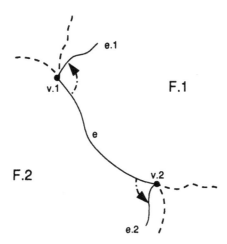

Figure 3.1: DCEL information stored in the record of edge e.

- the coordinates of v_i,

see Figure 3.1 for an illustration. Clearly, this data structure enables us to efficiently visit the edges incident with a given vertex of M in *counterclockwise* order, provided that a starting edge is available. Similarly, we can trace the edges bordering a given face of M in *clockwise* order if an initial edge is given. Either operation can be carried out in time proportional to the number of edges visited, see [52] or [51] for details.

Once the DCEL of a map M is available, the antipodal representation, organized with respect to the *clockwise* order of edges incident with a vertex, can be constructed in time $O(n)$, where n denotes the number of faces of M. Since we will need to scan face boundaries, and sets of edges radiating from a vertex, in both clockwise and counterclockwise direction, we shall incorporate both organization principles into one data structure (using two pointers per vertex in each edge record) that will subsequently be referred to as the D^2CEL of M. D^2CEL can be constructed from DCEL in time $O(n)$.

The data structure D^2CEL can as well be employed in storing the degenerate map $V(S)$. If (v, B) is a vertex of $V(S)$ where $v \notin \Gamma$ then the coordinate entry of (v, B) in each record of an edge incident with (v, B) contains the coordinates of v. In addition, we will store the name of the site, p, whose region contains v, with the coordinates of v. Note that these sites can easily be computed in time $O(n)$; we only have to traverse the edges incident with each vertex (in any order) and

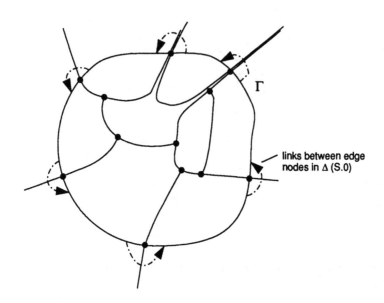

Figure 3.2: The order of the infinite borderlines.

determine the minimum site of all adjacent faces, due to Theorem 2.3.5. If $v \in \Gamma$ then each coordinate entry of (v, B) is blank.

Definition 3.1.1 The D^2CEL just defined is called the *representation of $V(S_0)$* and denoted by $\Delta(S_0)$.

Note that $\Delta(S_0)$ contains exactly the information on $V(S_0)$ we are interested in. First, it stores the coordinates of all vertices that are not lying over points of Γ, that is, of all vertices of $V(S_0)$. If e is an edge bordering two finite faces then its edge record contains the names, F_p and F_q, of the adjacent faces, and this allows the underlying curve segment β to be computed as a segment of $J(p, q)$. We neither want to locate vertices over points of Γ nor compute segments of Γ, because Γ is not part of the original diagram $V(S_0)$. But we shall use the *links* between those edges of $V(S)$ which represent the segments of Γ in $\Delta(S_0)$, in order to extract the cyclical order of the unbounded borderlines of $V(S_0)$ "at infinity", see Figure 3.2.

As a matter of fact, $\Delta(S_0)$ contains no extra links between different vertices that lie over the same point v.

3.2 The divide-and-conquer approach

In order to compute the representation, $\Delta(S_0)$, of $V(S_0)$ we shall employ an algorithmic paradigm called the *divide-and-conquer* technique. In this approach, a given problem is partioned into subproblems of smaller size that are solved separately. Then the solutions for the parts are merged into a solution for the original problem. This technique has been successfully applied to a variety of algorithmic problems [2] and, in particular, to problems in computational geometry [50]. Also, the first (time and space) optimal algorithm for constructing the Euclidean Voronoi diagram of n points in the plane presented in [56] was of divide-and-conquer type (cf. Section 1.1). The following recursive high-level description also applies to the general case studied in this book.

algorithm *construct* $\Delta(T_0)$; { *where $T_0 \subseteq S_0$ and $T_0 \neq \emptyset$*}
   if $|T_0| = 1$ **then** $\Delta(T_0) := \emptyset$
   else *divide T_0 into non-empty subsets L_0 and R_0;*
        construct $\Delta(L_0)$;
        construct $\Delta(R_0)$;
        merge $\Delta(L_0), \Delta(R_0)$ *giving* $\Delta(T_0)$
   end-if.

Suppose that both the divide and the merge operation can be carried out in $O(|T_0|)$ steps, in a fixed computation model. Then the above algorithm computes $\Delta(S_0)$ in $O(n \log n)$ steps, provided that in each divide step the subsets L_0 and R_0 of T_0 have about the same size. If $\alpha \leq |L_0|/|T_0| \leq 1 - \alpha$ holds for a global constant α in $(0, 1)$, then the tree reflecting the recursive partition of S_0 is a *weight-balanced* tree of height $O(\log n)$ (see Theorem 2, Chap. III. 5.1, in [42]) to each of whose levels an $O(n)$ computation cost must be charged.

In the Euclidean case, the n sites in S_0 can first be sorted according to the lexicographic order of their coordinates; this can be done in time $O(n \log n)$ (see [42]). Then each divide step can be carried out in time $O(|T_0|)$, using a horizontal or a vertical line to divide T_0 into subsets whose cardinality is between 1/4 and 3/4 times the size of T_0, up to one point.

The difficulty is with the merge step. Let $S_0 = L_0 \cup R_0$ be a partition of S_0 into non-empty subsets. Let $L := L_0 \cup \{\infty\}$, and $R := R_0 \cup \{\infty\}$. Suppose that $\Delta(S_0)$ has already been constructed. Each bounded face of $V(S)$ belongs either to a site of L_0, or to a site of R_0. Correspondingly, there are three types of edges in $V(S)$ both of whose adjacent faces are finite: those who are common border of two L_0-faces, or of two R_0-faces, and the set $J(L_0, R_0)$ of those edges bordering an L_0-face and an R_0-face, see Figure 3.3.

Definition 3.2.1 The set of edges $J(L_0, R_0)$ is called the *bisector* of the subsets L_0 and R_0 of S_0. Each edge e in $J(L_0, R_0)$ is assumed to be *oriented* in such a way that the L_0-face adjacent to e is on the left.

Let e be an edge of the first type that borders the faces F_{p_1} and F_{p_2}, where $p_1, p_2 \in L_0$. Assume $p_1 < p_2$. Then e corresponds to a maximal borderline (β, p_1, p_2), where $\beta \subset R(p_1, S) \cap \overline{R(p_2, S)} \subset J(p_1, p_2)$. A fortiori, $\beta \subset R(p_1, L) \cap \overline{R(p_2, L)}$. Thus, there exists a borderline $(\hat{\beta}, p_1, p_2)$ in $V(L)$ such that $\beta \subseteq \hat{\beta}$, that is, e is contained in an edge $\hat{e}$ of $V(L)$. Assume that, in $V(L)$, $\hat{e}$ extends beyond the end-vertex (v, B) of e in $V(S)$, as shown in Figure 3.4. Since (v, B) is of degree ≥ 3, besides the regions of p_1 and p_2 at least one more region, $R(q, S)$, is adjacent to (v, B). If q were in L then v would induce a vertex of $V(L)$, causing $\hat{e}$ to terminate. Thus, $q \in R_0$. Consequently, the point (v, B) is passed by the bisector $J(L_0, R_0)$. The same holds for edges of $V(S)$ that are bordering two R_0-faces.

This shows that our main task is to *compute the bisector* $J(L_0, R_0)$. Namely, these edges are not represented in $\Delta(L_0)$, nor in $\Delta(R_0)$, but need to be incorporated into $\Delta(S_0)$. Second, the course of $J(L_0, R_0)$ determines where to correctly cut the edges of $V(L)$ and $V(R)$, in order to obtain those edges of $V(S)$ that separate faces of the same type; cf. Figure 1.3.

$J(L_0, R_0)$ shall be computed by tracing successive edges. The problems are *where to begin, how to determine the end-vertex of a bisecting edge, and how to continue computation if a vertex with more than two incident edges of $J(L_0, R_0)$ is encountered.*

In merging Euclidean Voronoi diagrams, the last problem does not occur because the bisector of two finite, non-empty point sets, that are separated by a vertical line, consists of one y-monotone polygonal chain, see [52] and Figure 1.3. The second problem is the hardest one; in Section 3.4.1 we will briefly recall the solution in the Euclidean case, before turning to abstract Voronoi diagrams. The first problem of finding a starting edge is usually solved by recursively maintaining *convex hulls*; the two unbounded ends of the bisecting polygonal chain are the perpendicular bisectors of the two line segments that support the convex hulls of L_0 and R_0 (loc. cit.). As Chew and Drysdale [14] have pointed out, computing the

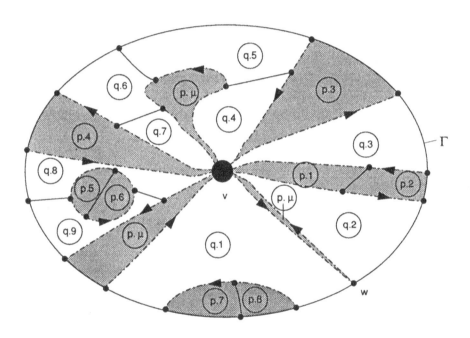

Figure 3.3: The bisector $J(L_0, R_0)$. L_0-faces are denoted by p_i, R_0-faces by q_j.

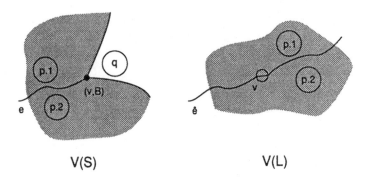

V(S)   V(L)

Figure 3.4: In $V(S)$, edge e terminates at (v, B).

convex hull is unnecessary: Since one knows that two elements of $J(L_0, R_0)$ tend to infinity, it is sufficient to scan the non-empty intersections $R(p, L_0) \cap R(q, R_0)$ of the unbounded Voronoi regions for a segment of $J(p, q)$ contained therein. This can be accomplished in time proportional to the total number of infinite curve segments in $V(L_0)$ and $V(R_0)$.

As Figure 3.3 shows, $J(L_0, R_0)$ can contain connected components none of whose edges extends to Γ (that is, to infinity). Since it is not clear how to find starting segments for these components efficiently, the first problem (where to start) is solved by excluding such cases from consideration.

Definition 3.2.2 A partition of S_0 into non-empty subsets L_0 and R_0 is called *acyclic* iff for all non-empty subsets $L_0' \subseteq L_0$ and $R_0' \subseteq R_0$ the bisector $J(L_0', R_0')$ contains no cycle of (undirected, pairwise different) edges that avoids Γ.

Example The partition depicted in Figure 3.3 is not acyclic because the contour of $F_{p_5} \cup F_{p_6}$ is a forbidden cycle. The boundary of F_{p_μ} is a minimal edge cycle (*three* points are induced by v), but not a forbidden one because it contains points of Γ.

For later use we note the following.

Remark 3.2.3 *Let C be an edge cycle as in the above definition, that encircles a minimum number of faces. Then no vertex of $V(S)$ occurs twice in C, and all the faces encircled belong either to L_0 or to R_0.*

Now we turn to the second problem of how to organize the the computation of $J(L_0, R_0)$. We shall employ the following scheme which makes use of the fact that the borderlines radiating from a point of $V(S)$ are *ordered* (cf. Theorem 2.3.5). The term "outgoing" refers to the natural orientation of edges in $J(L_0, R_0)$ introduced in Definition 3.2.1.

algorithm *compute* $J(L_0, R_0)$; { *where* $S_0 = L_0 \cup R_0$ *is acyclic*}
scan Γ *clockwise for first outgoing borderline* $\beta_\infty \in J(L_0, R_0)$;
mark b_∞;
repeat
    $b := b_\infty$;
        determine endpoint v *of* b *in* $V(S)$;
        while v **not** *on* Γ **do**
            if v *in* L_0*- region* **then**
                determine next borderline $b \in J(L_0, R_0)$ *outgoing*
                from v *in counterclockwise direction*
            else {v *in* R_0*-region*}
                determine next borderline $b \in J(L_0, R_0)$ *outgoing*
                from v *in clockwise direction*
            end-if;
            determine endpoint v *of* b *in* $V(S)$
        end-while;
    scan Γ *clockwise for next outgoing borderline* $b_\infty \in J(L_0, R_0)$
until b_∞ *is marked.*

Figure 3.5 gives an example of how the algorithm works when started at the point i of Γ. Note that in the last line but one, the outgoing borderline clockwise next to old b_∞ is addressed. Since the central point, v (cf. Figure 3.3) belongs to the L_0-region $R(p_\mu, S)$, counterclockwise-first continuations are chosen whenever v is encountered as the endpoint of a borderline.

The orientation in which Γ is scanned is arbitrary. Crucial is the choice of orientation in the inner **while**-loop where the continuations are determined. If v is the endpoint of borderline b then we want b and the continuing borderline, b', to be incident with the same vertex of $V(S)$ induced by v. This is in fact achieved by the above algorithm. For, let $v \in R(p_\mu, S)$ where $p_\mu \in L_0$. Then the "pieces of pie" traversed on a counterclockwise march around v from b to b' must all belong to R_0-regions, and can, therefore, not be contained in $R(p_\mu, S)$. Thus, b and b' belong to the same vertex (v, B), cf. Theorem 2.3.5 and Definition 2.5.1. Consequently, we might as well replace the terms "borderline" and "point" with "edge" and "vertex" (with respect to $V(S)$) in the above algorithm.

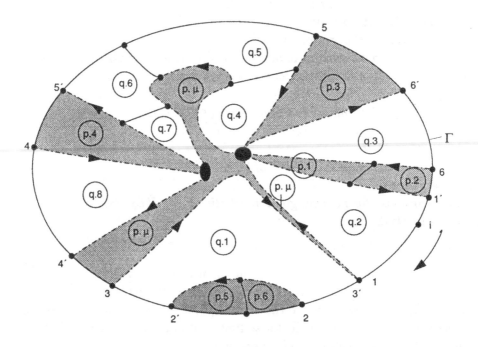

Figure 3.5: Computing $J(L_0, R_0)$.

3.3 Bisecting chains

During the i-th execution of the **repeat**-loop in the algorithm *compute* an *oriented path* K_i is computed in the planar map $V(S)$, that consists only of edges of the bisector $J(L_0, R_0)$. K_i connects two (possibly identical) vertices on Γ; but no vertex in the interior domain of Γ can occur in K_i twice, because the partition $S_0 = L_0 \cup R_0$ is acyclic. Therefore, K_i is *simple* (as a path in a map, not necessarily as a curve).

Let e be an edge in $J(L_0, R_0)$; e can be continued in both directions, using the strategy of the algorithm (when tracing edges opposed to their orientation, "clockwise" must be interchanged with "counterclockwise"). Since no edge circle can result this way, either continuation must eventually reach the curve Γ. Thus, e is contained in a path K_i. *This shows that the above algorithm correctly computes $J(L_0, R_0)$.*

Definition 3.3.1 Each path K_i that is computed by algorithm *compute* is called a *bisecting chain*. Let $\mathcal{L}_i$ (resp. $\mathcal{R}_i$) denote the union of all Voronoi regions *on the left* (resp. *on the right*) of K_i. Finally, let $\mathcal{L}$ (resp. $\mathcal{R}$) the union of the L_0-*regions* (the R_0-regions). See Figure 3.6 for an illustration.

If two chains have a vertex (v, B) in common they *do not cross* at (v, B). Figure 3.7 shows different cases that arise from a path K_j meeting a path K_i constructed in a previous step. Only the second case applies; here an edge continuing K_j is encountered before the incoming edge of K_i is reached. The case where K_j meets K_i from the other side is symmetric. It also follows that K_i and K_j are *edge-disjoint* if $i \neq j$.

Lemma 3.3.2   *1. Let v be a point of the curve K_i with admissible neighborhood U. If $v \in \mathcal{L}$ then $U \cap \mathcal{R}_i \subset \mathcal{R}$ and, therefore, $v \in \mathcal{L}_i$. A symmetric assertion holds if $v \in \mathcal{R}$.*

2. If $K_i \neq K_j$ then $K_i \subset \mathcal{L}_j$ or $K_i \subset \mathcal{R}_j$.

Proof: 1. Assume $v \notin \Gamma$ and $v \in \mathcal{L}$. Each time the point v is passed by a curve K_i the part of U on the right of this curve segment is fully contained in $\mathcal{R}$ because prolongations are determined in counterclockwise order; see Figure 3.8. This implies assertion 1). An inspection of Figure 2.11 shows that 1) also holds for $v \in \Gamma$.

2. Even where K_i touches K_i, the membership of points of K_i in $\mathcal{L}_j$ (or $\mathcal{R}_i$) does not change. $\square$

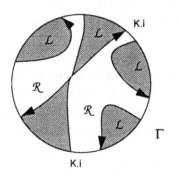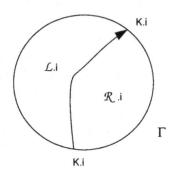

Figure 3.6: The notations of Definition 3.3.1.

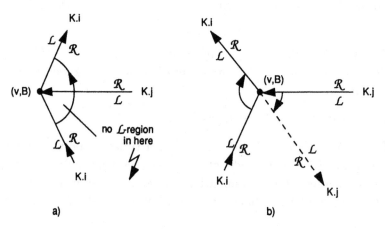

Figure 3.7: Different chains do not cross. In case a): $v \in \mathcal{L}$, in case b): $v \in \mathcal{R}$.

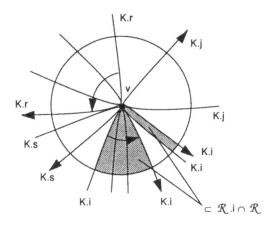

Figure 3.8: Bisecting chains meeting at a point $v \in \mathcal{L}$.

The bisecting chains in $J(L_0, R_0)$ are chopping those pieces off a region $R(p, L)$ that do not belong to $R(p, S)$.

Lemma 3.3.3 *For each $p \in L_0$ (and, symmetrically, for points of R_0) the following assertions hold.*

1. $R(p, S) = R(p, L) \cap \bigcap\limits_{p \in L_j} \mathcal{L}_j$.

2. *If the intersection $R(p, L) \cap \mathcal{L}_j$ is not empty then it contains p and is path-connected.*

Proof: 1. "$\subseteq$" follows directly from Definition 3.3.1. "$\supseteq$": Let z belong to the right hand side. If $z \notin R(p, S)$ then $z \in R(q, S)$ for a site $q \neq p$. Since $z \in R(p, L)$ the site q must belong to R_0. Let K_j be a bisecting chain such that F_p is on the left of K_j, and F_q on the right. By assumption, $z \in \mathcal{L}_j$, which contradicts $z \in R(q, S) \subset \mathcal{R}_j$.

2. Let $z \in R(p, L) \cap \mathcal{L}_j$, and let $\alpha \subset R(p, L)$ be an arc connecting p with z. If $\alpha \subset \mathcal{L}_j$ the assertions follow. Otherwise, α contains points of the bisecting chain K_j. Let v be last point of K_j on α, as counting from p. If $v \neq z$ then the segment $\alpha|_{(v,z]}$ is contained in $\mathcal{L}_j$.

Assume first that $v \in R(p, S)$. Then, by Lemma 3.3.2, 1), $v \in \mathcal{L}_j$ and $R(p, S) \subset \mathcal{L}_j$. Let β be an arc in $R(p, S)$ from p to v; then β followed by $\alpha|_{[v,z]}$ is an arc in $R(p, L) \cap \mathcal{L}_j$.

Now suppose that $v \notin R(p, S)$. Since $v \in R(p, L)$ this implies $v \in R(q, S)$, where $q \in R_0$. By Lemma 3.3.2, $v \in \mathcal{R}_j$, which shows $v \neq z$. Let U be an admissible neighborhood of v, see Figure 3.9. If $v' \in \alpha|_{(v,z]}$ is close enough to v then $\alpha|_{(v,v')} \subset U \cap \mathcal{L}_j \subset \mathcal{L}$, by Lemma 3.3.2. Since $\alpha \subset R(p,L)$ this means $\alpha|_{(v,v')} \subset R(p,S) \cap \mathcal{L}_j$. Then the whole of $R(p,S)$ is contained in $\mathcal{L}_j$. Let $w \in \alpha|_{(v,v')}$, and let β be an arc in $R(p,S)$ connecting p with w. Then the concatenation of β and $\alpha_{[w,z]}$ is the desired arc in $R(p,L) \cap \mathcal{L}_j$ that connects p with z. $\square$

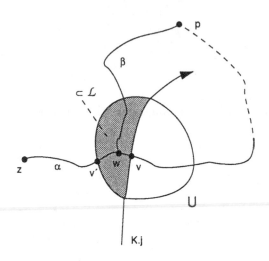

Figure 3.9: Illustration of the proof of Lemma 3.3.3. Point v belongs to $\mathcal{R}_j$, and β is contained in $R(p,S)$

This lemma places restrictions on how a region $R(p,L)$ can be intersected by a bisecting chain. The situations displayed in Figure 3.10, for example, cannot occur, due to assertion 2).

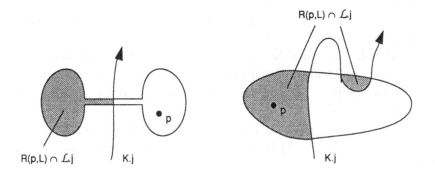

Figure 3.10: No chain can intersect $R(p,L)$ like K_j does.

In the following sections we are refining the algorithm *compute* given above. This will be done in two steps. First, we confine ourselves to the non-degenerate case where any two bisecting curves may only *cross* at a point, but not touch one another (Section 3.4). A complete description of the merge algorithm is given, and its performance is evaluated. In a second step (Section 3.5) it is shown how to adapt the algorithm to degenerate Voronoi diagrams.

3.4 The non-degenerate case

Throughout this section we assume: if any two bisecting curves, $J(p,q)$ and $J(p',q')$ of $\mathcal{J}_0$, have a point v in common then they properly cross at v, as depicted in Figure 3.11.

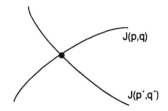

Figure 3.11: A proper cross-point.

As a consequence, all Voronoi diagrams $V(S')$, where $S' \subseteq S$, are regular, so we need not distinguish points from induced points.

3.4.1 Determining endpoints of chain segments

Suppose that during the execution of the algorithm *compute* (see Section 3.2) a borderline

$$b = (\beta, \{p,q\}) \in J(L_0, R_0)$$

has been computed that goes out from a point v. Here $p \in L_0, q \in R_0, \beta \subset J(p,q)$, and $J(p,q)$ is oriented such that p is on the left. The next and crucial step in the algorithm is determining the endpoint, v', of b in $V(S)$. This problem is dealt with in the present subsection.

Fortunately, the problem of determining v' can be divided among $V(L)$ and $V(R)$.

Lemma 3.4.1.1 *Let v_L and v_R denote the endpoints of b in $V(L \cup \{q\})$ and in $V(\{p\} \cup R)$, correspondingly. Then v' is the first one of v_L, v_R on $J(p,q)$ after v.*

The proof follows the line of the remarks connected with Figure 3.4 (after Definition 3.2.1). In order to determine v_L, assume that the predecessor borderline in the bisecting chain K containing b is not a p-borderline, too.

In the Euclidean case, this means that b is entering the region $R(p,L)$ at the point v, see Figure 3.12. Assume that $R(p,L)$ is bounded. Since this region is *convex*, the halfline continuing b meets the contour of $R(p,L)$ *in exactly one point* that must be equal to v_L because, after leaving $R(p,L)$, $J(p,q)$ is no longer a p-borderline in $V(L \cup \{q\})$. The point v_L can be determined by *scanning* the boundary edges of $R(p,L)$ for the unique point of intersection with $J(p,q)|_{(v,\infty)}$. Suppose that the endpoint of b in $V(\{p\} \cup R)$, v_R, is closer to v than v_L is. Then b terminates in v_R, and a new p-borderline, b_2, starts; if v_R is an inner point of an edge $\subset J(q,q_2)$ in $V(R)$ then b_2 is a $\{p,q_2\}$-borderline. Now the endpoints of b_2 in $V(L \cup \{q_2\})$ and $V(\{p\} \cup R)$, $v_{L,2}$ and $v_{R,2}$, must be determined. Again, $v_{L,2}$ is the unique point of intersection of $J(p,q_2)|_{(v_R,\infty)}$ and the contour of $R(p,L)$. Because the right halfplane of $J(p,q)$ cannot contain points of $R(p,S)$ the borderline b_2 has to *turn left* when starting from v_R. The bisecting curves being straight lines, $J(p,q)|_{(v_R,\infty)}$ and $J(p,q_2)|_{(v_R,\infty)}$ do *not cross* before meeting $\partial R(p,L)$. Therefore, $v_{L,2}$ comes between v_L and v with respect to the *counterclockwise order* on the boundary of $R(p,L)$. More generally, if b is followed by p-borderlines $b_2, \ldots, b_j$ in the bisecting chain K then the points $v, v_L, v_{L,2}, \ldots, v_{L,j}$ are in counterclockwise order. Thus, they can be determined by scanning the contour of $R(p,L)$ counterclockwise, without backtracking.

This *scan principle* is the core of the algorithm presented in [56]. Because the boundary of a region can be scanned in time proportional to the number of edges (using the D^2CEL representation of $V(L_0)$, cf. Section 3.1), the whole merge step can be carried out in time $O(n)$, where n is the number of sites. This results in an optimal $O(n \log n)$ algorithm for computing the Euclidean Voronoi diagram (cf. Section 3.2).

With abstract Voronoi diagrams the following difficulties arise. First, a point of intersection with the boundary of $R(p,L)$ does not necessarily cause a p-borderline to end, if the curves merely touch each other. This problem is dealt with in

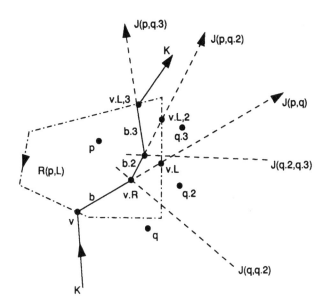

Figure 3.12: Computing the bisecting chain in the Euclidean case.

Section 3.5. Second, the contour of $\partial R(p, L)$ can be crossed several times by the continuation of borderline b, so that it is not obvious how to detect the right point of crossing (i.e., the first one after v on $J(p,q)$). Third, the segments of $J(p, q_i)$ and $J(p, q_{i+1})$ emanating from $v_{R,i}$ may cross before meeting the contour of $R(p, L)$, thereby destroying the counterclockwise order; see Figure 3.13. None of these problems has been addressed in [14].

Let $b_j, b_{j+1}, \ldots, b_r$ be a sequence of consecutive edges of chain K. If all of these edges are p-borderlines then the site p is said to be *active* during the computation of $b_j, \ldots, b_r$. In contradistinction to the Euclidean case, a site can be active several times.

Definition 3.4.1.2 Let b denote a $\{p,q\}$-borderline segment in the bisecting chain K, with starting-point v and endpoint w. Then w is called a *p-exit point of K* iff w is endpoint of b in $V(L \cup \{q\})$. The point v is called a *p-entry point of K* iff one of the following conditions is fulfilled.

1. b is the first segment in K.

2. The predecessor segment of b in K is not a p-borderline.

3. v is a p-exit point of K.

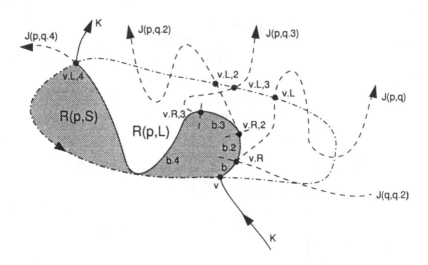

Figure 3.13: Potential problems with bisecting chains in abstract Voronoi diagrams.

Figure 3.14 gives an example of the third case. Here, $L_0 = \{p, p'\}$, $R_0 = \{q, q'\}$, and $q = \min(L_0 \cup R_0)$, so that chain continuations are determined clockwise.

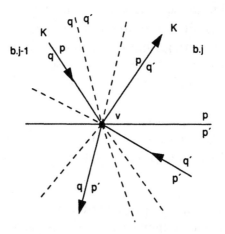

Figure 3.14: Point v is both a p-entry and p-exit point of K.

To solve the above problems, we first prove a result on the order of the points of intersection of two simple curves which can be formulated quite naturally for curves on the sphere.

Lemma 3.4.1.3 *For $i = 1, 2$, let C_i be a simple closed, oriented curve on the sphere. Let L_i and R_i denote the domains on the left and on the right of C_i, correspondingly. Assume that $C_1 \cap C_2$ consists of m proper cross-points, where $2 \leq m < \infty$. Then the following assertions are equivalent.*

1. *$L_1 \cap L_2$ is connected.*

2. *$R_1 \cap R_2$ is connected.*

3. *The points of $C_1 \cap C_2$ are in the same order on either curve.*

Proof: The surface of the sphere, S^2, is dissected by $C_1 \cup C_2$ into finitely many domains each of whose boundaries is a simple closed curve consisting of segments of C_1 alternating with segments of C_2 (because $C_1 \cap C_2$ contains at least two cross-points). If the boundary of domain D contains a segment of C_i that is counterclockwise oriented with respect to D then $D \subset L_i$; consequently, *each segment of C_i in ∂D must be counterclockwise oriented*. Thus, to the four types of domains (those contained in $L_1 \cap L_2$, $L_1 \cap R_2$, $R_1 \cap L_2$, or in $R_1 \cap R_2$) four boundary types correspond, see Figure 3.15. Let $D \subset L_i$, and assume that σ_1 and σ_2 are C_i-segments of ∂D that are successive on C_i (that is, having left σ_1, the curve C_i doesn't visit any other segment of ∂D before passing through σ_2). Then the part of ∂D between the endpoint of σ_1 and the starting point of σ_2 is disjoint from C_i, see Figure 3.16. Thus, σ_1 and σ_2 are successive on ∂D, too.

Now assume that assertion 1) holds. Suppose there were a domain $D \subset L_1 \cap R_2$ whose boundary contains more than one segment of C_1 or of C_2; then ∂D contains at least two segments of each. Let ρ_1 and ρ_2 be two segments of C_2. By the above, the C_1-segments preceding and following ρ_j on ∂D are joined directly by some arc α_j of C_1. Together with α_j, the segment ρ_j forms a counterclockwise oriented cycle Z_j, see Figure 3.17. The domains encircled by Z_1 and by Z_2 are disjoint. Each of them may be trespassed by the curve C_2 finitely often, but each time a cycle is bisected by an oriented arc one of the resulting subdomains has again a cyclic contour of the same orientation. Thus, there are at least two domains in $S^2 - (C_1 \cup C_2)$ whose boundaries are counterclockwise oriented - a contradiction to 1). Therefore, *the contour of each component of $L_1 \cap R_2$ (or of $L_2 \cap R_1$), consists of two segments only, one of C_1 and one of C_2.* Now let $v, w \in C_1 \cap C_2$ be two successive points of C_1. The two domains adjacent to the arc α of C_1 that connects v with w cannot both have a cyclic contour, see Figure 3.18. One of them being acyclic, v and w are directly connected by an arc of C_2 that has the same orientation as α, by the above. This implies 3). With the same proof, 2) yields 3). Conversely, if 3) holds then only one component, D, of $S^2 - (C_1 \cup C_2)$ can have a clockwise (resp. counterclockwise) cyclical contour since it takes all of C_1 and

C_2 to connect the points of $C_1 \cap C_2$ contained in the contour of D by double arcs. □

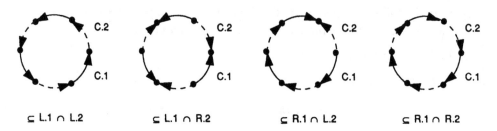

$$\subseteq L.1 \cap L.2 \qquad \subseteq L.1 \cap R.2 \qquad \subseteq R.1 \cap L.2 \qquad \subseteq R.1 \cap R.2$$

Figure 3.15: Four different boundary types.

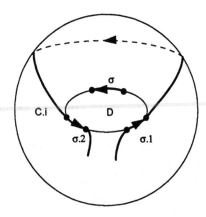

Figure 3.16: Segment σ is not contained in C_i.

If applied to the counterclockwise oriented contour of $R(p, L)$ and to $J(p, q)$, the above lemma yields that no bounded clockwise oriented cycle can arise from these two curves in the plane (because $R(p, L \cup \{q\})$ is connected, only one such cycle exists after taking projection onto the sphere; this cycle must contain the pole). Hence, *the endpoint v_L of the borderline b in $V(L \cup \{q\})$ must be the first point of $J(p, q)|_{(v, \infty)} \cap \partial R(p, L)$ that is encountered when tracing the contour of $R(p, L)$ counterclockwise from v.* That is, $J(p, q)$ cannot run as displayed in Figure 3.13. Another consequence is that the p-entry points and p-exit points of a bisecting chain on a region contour are ordered (Lemma 3.3.3, 2). In the case displayed in Figure 3.14 v is conceptually resolved into a p-exit and a p-entry point).

This leaves us with the problem of p-borderline continuations that *cross* before

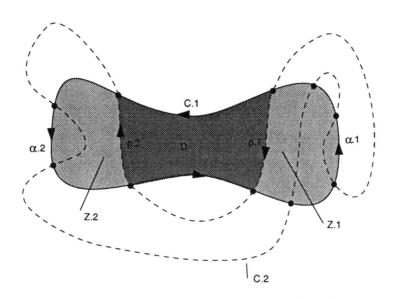

Figure 3.17: Two counterclockwise oriented cycles.

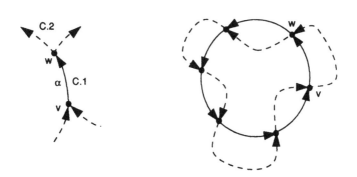

Figure 3.18: An impossible situation, and the only possible one.

meeting the contour of $R(p, L)$, see $J(p, q_2)$ and $J(p, q_3)$ in Figure 3.13. Here a solution can be based upon the following oberservation illustrated by Figure 3.19.

Lemma 3.4.1.4 *Let $p \in L$, $q' \in R$, and let b' be a $\{p, q'\}$-borderline with respect to S that emanates from v'. Assume that $J(p, q')|_{(v', \infty)}$ crosses a bisecting curve $J(p, q'')$ at the point v'', where $q'' \in R$. Then b' does not extend further than v'' as a borderline in $V(\{p\} \cup R)$.*

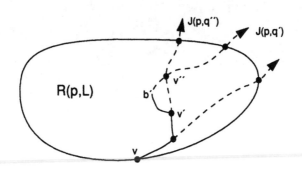

Figure 3.19: The $\{p, q'\}$-borderline b' ends not later than at v''.

Proof: Having changed into $D(q'', p)$, $J(p, q')$ can no longer be contained in the region $\overline{R(p, \{p\} \cup R)}$.   □

Thus, if we know that the prolongation of b' meets a bisecting curve $J(p, q'')$ before meeting the contour of $R(p, L)$ then we need not determine the endpoint v'_L of b' in $V(L \cup \{q'\})$ because its endpoint v'_R in $V(\{p\} \cup R)$ comes first and, by Lemma 3.4.1.1, equals the endpoint of b' in $V(S)$.

The following algorithm takes advantage of this fact by maintaining a *test segment* T that will be checked before the contour of $R(p, L)$ is scanned. The algorithm is given as a function *L-endpoint* of the parameters $(p, q, v,$ entry-point, $T)$ in pseudo-Pascal notation. It will only be called if $p \in L_0, q \in R_0$, and if $J(p, q)$ passes v and gives rise to a $\{p, q\}$-borderline b with respect to S "shortly after" v. The variable parameter T will not be accessed from the outside of the function; it merely serves as permanent memory. Along with T, its starting-point $T.s$, its endpoint $T.e$, and the site $T.r$ such that $T \subset J(p, T.r)$ are assumed to be available. The value of *entry-point* is supposed to be *true* iff v is a p-entry point when $L(p, q, v,$ entry-point, $T)$ is invoked, see Definition 3.4.1.2.

Here and in the following, the representations $\Delta(L_0)$ and $\Delta(R_0)$ are *global objects*. To either one, pointers are maintained that move whenever region boundaries, or edges incident with a vertex, are scanned. Two pointers, λ_∞ and ρ_∞, are used for tracing the augmenting curves of $V(L)$ and $V(R)$, whereas λ and ρ are used for tracing the bisecting chains. We will, however, not explicitly refer to these pointers if their usage is obvious.

```
1)    function L-endpoint (p, q : site; v : point; entry-point: boolean;
          var T: curve segment): point;
2)    var v_L : point;
3)          done : boolean;
4)    begin
5)          done := false;
6)          if not entry-point then
7)              if v ∈ T then
8)                  T.s := v;
9)                  if q = T.r then
10)                     L-endpoint := T.e;
11)                     done := true
12)                 end-if
13)             end-if;
14)             if (not done) and (T crossed by J(p, q)|_(v,∞) before T.e) then
15)                 L-endpoint := ∞_2;
16)                 done := true
17)             end-if;
18)         else {v is a p-entry point}
19)             T.e := v
20)         end-if;
21)         if not done then
22)             scan ∂R(p, L) counterclockwise from T.e for first point
23)                 v_L crossed by J(p, q)|_(v,∞);
24)             L-endpoint := v_L;
25)             T := J(p, q)|_[v,v_L];
26)         end-if
27)   end-function
```

Let $b_i, \ldots, b_r$ be a sequence of consecutive edges in the bisecting chain K, where each b_l is a $\{p, q_l\}$-borderline with respect to S. Let v_l denote the starting-point of b_l, and assume that v_i is the only p-entry point.

Theorem 3.4.1.5 *Suppose that the function L-endpoint* (p, q_l, v_l, e_l, T) *is called for* $l = i, \ldots, r$, *in this order, where* $e_i = $ *true and* $e_l = $ *false for* $l > i$. *Then each call either returns the endpoint* $v_{L,l}$ *of* b_l *in* $V(L \cup \{q_l\})$, *or the symbol* ∞_2. *In the latter case,* $v_{R,l}$ *is closer to* v_l *than* $v_{L,l}$ *on* $J(p, q_l)$. *During execution of these function calls, the contour of* $R(p, L)$ *is scanned counterclockwise, with no backtracking.*

Proof: By induction on l. In addition, we show that the following invariant holds for the segment T after the execution of *L-endpoint* (p, q_l, v_l, e_l, T) has terminated.

∗) T is a continuation of the last borderline $b_j, i \leq j \leq l$, for which $v_{L,j}$ has been computed in line 10 or 24. We have $T.e = v_{L,j}$. The point $T.s$ is the last point of $v_i, \ldots, v_l$ contained in $J(p, T.r)$.

See Figure 3.20 for an illustration.

Suppose that *L-endpoint* $(p, q_i, v_i, \text{true}, T)$ is being invoked. Since v_i is a p-entry point, the contour of $R(p, L)$ is scanned from v_i counterclockwise for the first point crossed by $J(p, q_i)|_{(v, \infty)}$ which we know to be equal to $v_{L,i}$ (lines 19, 21–24). Then the test segment T is initially defined to be the part of $J(p, q_i)$ between v_i and $v_{L,i}$ (line 25). Hereby, all assertions are fulfilled.

Now suppose that *L-endpoint* $(p, q_l, v_l, \text{false}, T)$ is being called, where $i < l$. Point v_l is contained in the continuation of the borderline b_{l-1} considered in the previous step. If v_l lies on the current segment T then T's starting-point is updated (line 8) according to the invariant ∗). Should, in addition, the borderline b_l be part of T we need not search for $v_{L,l} = T.e$ (lines 9–12); this case can occur if the site $T.r$ becomes active again (see the upper drawing of Figure 3.20, assuming that current b extends as far as to the point of intersection with T, such that the next borderline can again be of $\{p, T.r\}$-type). Otherwise, it is first tested whether T is crossed by $J(p, q_l)|_{(v_l, \infty)}$ before its endpoint, $T.e$. If this is the case, the value ∞_2 is assigned to the function (lines 14,15), and we must prove the following.

Claim The point $v_{R,l}$ comes before $v_{L,l}$ on $J(p, q_l)$.

Proof: To apply Lemma 3.4.1.4, we must show that $J(p, q_l)|_{(v_l, \infty)}$ does not cross the contour of $R(p, L)$ before crossing T. Let f be the first point of $\partial R(p, L)$ on $J(p, q_l)$ after v_l. For short, let $q_j := T.r$, $J := J(p, q_j)$, and let J_T be the component of $R(p, L) \cap J$ that contains T, see Figure 3.21. $R(p, L)$ is bisected by J_T into two domains; let D denote the domain on the right hand side of J_T.

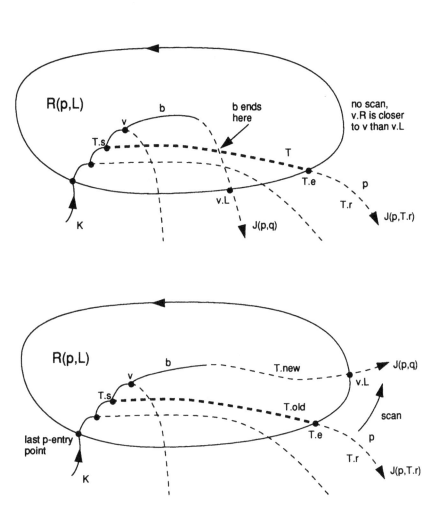

Figure 3.20: The use of test segment T.

If point f belongs to the boundary of D then $J(p, q_l)$ must cross T in order to get to f. For, $J(p, q_l)$ cannot cross itself, nor one of the foregoing borderlines, $b_j, \ldots, b_{l-1}$, nor the part of J before b_j from the p-side first, because this would contradict the general assumption that the partition $S_0 = L_0 \cup R_0$ is acyclic (Definition 3.2.2). See Figure 3.22, where the encircled domain must in fact contain $R(p, \{p\} \cup \{q_j, \ldots, q_l\})$ since the b_k are known to be p-borderlines with respect even to S.

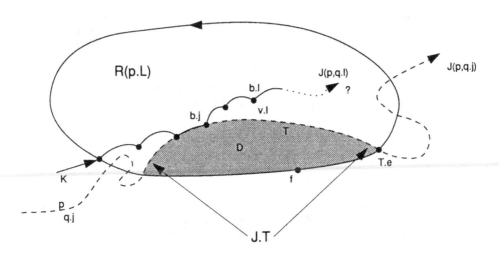

Figure 3.21: Notations.

Now assume that $f \notin \partial D$. Then $J(p, q_l)|_{(v_l, \infty)}$ cannot cross the test segment T at all. For, in addition to the restriction just mentioned, no piece of $J(p, q_l)$ can form a clockwise oriented cycle with a piece of the contour of $R(p, L)$; see Figure 3.23. Hereby, the claim is proven.   □

The proof of the theorem is continued with the case that T is *not* crossed by $J(p, q_l)|_{(v_l, \infty)}$ before $T.e$. Then the contour of $R(p, L)$ is scanned counterclockwise from $T.e$ (lines 21–23) for the first point crossed by $J(p, q_l)|_{(v_l, \infty)}$. This point must in fact equal $v_{L,l}$, the first point of $\partial R(p, L)$ on $J(p, q_l)$ after v_l. For, after leaving $R(p, L)$ at f, $J(p, q_l)|_{(v_l, \infty)}$ cannot get to the piece of $\partial R(p, L)$ running from $T.e$ to f; see Figure 3.23 and Figure 3.24. Thus, line 24 is correct, and updating T (line 25) restores invariant *). Clearly, the contour of $R(p, L)$ was never walked clockwise. This completes the proof of the theorem.   □

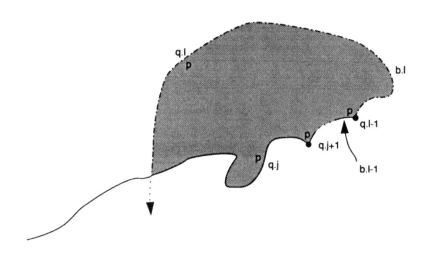

Figure 3.22: A forbidden cycle caused in $J(L_0', R_0')$ where $L_0' = \{p\}$, $R_0' = \{q_j, \ldots, q_l\}$.

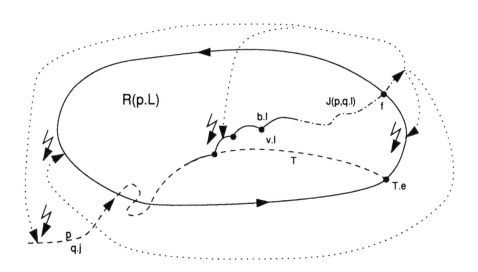

Figure 3.23: $J(p, q_l)$ cannot get to T.

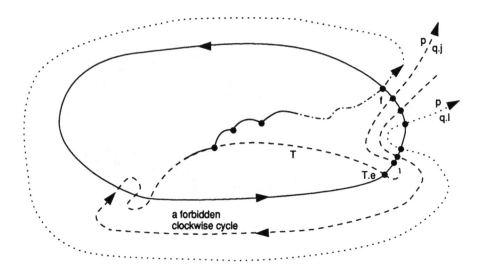

Figure 3.24: An impossible situation

As to the implementation, scanning the contour of $R(p, L)$ is enabled by the D^2CEL representation of $V(L_0)$ (cf. Definition 3.1.1). During the scan to be performed in line 22 of function L-endpoint, only those edges of $\partial R(p, L)$ whose other adjacent face is finite are actually searched for the first point crossed by $J(p, q)|_{(v, \infty)}$. If an edge $e \subset \Gamma$ is encountered, we do not compute intersections but test whether $J(p, q)|_{(v, \infty)}$ is *between* the adjacent continuations, π and σ, of the predecessor and the successor edge of e in $\partial R(p, L)$ "at infinity", see Figure 3.25. If this is the case, v_L is assigned the value ∞_1 which is defined to be less than ∞_2, the value returned in line 15. If v_R is of value ∞_1, too, this marks the end of the currently computed bisecting chain. If $J(p, q)$ intersects π, or σ, then the first point of intersection becomes the new $T.e$, as usual.

Both of the above operations, searching a bisecting curve for a point crossed by another bisecting curve, and testing "betweenness at infinity", can be performed in time $O(1)$ in the Euclidean case, all bisecting curves being straight lines. If nothing is known about the curves, both problems can become arbitrarly complex. For example, if the curves are derived from the graphs of primitive recursive functions by interpolation, testing for intersection becomes undecidable. Since we are interested in the complexity of constructing Voronoi diagrams *relative* to these elementary operations, we are adding them as primitives to the model of computation. The details are given in Definition 3.4.3.1 below.

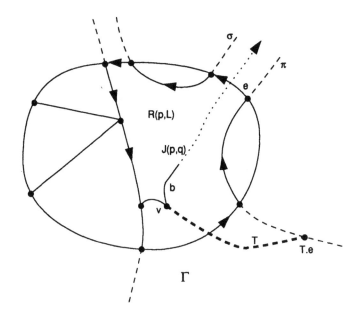

Figure 3.25: Testing edges contained in Γ.

Symmetrically to the function L-*endpoint*, a function R-*endpoint* is defined. In the corresponding line 22, $\partial R(q, R)$ is scanned *clockwise*. Now the statement "determine endpoint v of b in $V(S)$" of algorithm *compute* in Section 3.2, that refers to a $\{p, q\}$-borderline b w.r.t. S emanating from a point v_0, can be refined as follows.

$$v_L := L\text{-}endpoint\ (p, q, v_0, e_L, T_L);$$
$$v_R := R\text{-}endpoint\ (p, q, v_0, e_R, T_R);$$
$$v := \min(v_L, v_R);$$
$$e_L := (v_L \leq v_R);$$
$$e_R := (v_R \leq v_L);$$
$$\textbf{if}\ \ v = \infty_1\ \textbf{then}\ v\text{-on-}\Gamma := true;$$

The boolean variables e_L and e_R are assumed to be set correctly before the function calls; at least one of them has the value *true*. Therefore, at most one of v_L, v_R, is assigned the value ∞_2 which, by convention, is the maximum of all possible values. For finite v_L, v_R, the order on the oriented curve $J(p, q)$ is being referred to. Deciding which one comes first requires a further elementary operation; see Definition 3.4.3.1.

Theorem 3.4.1.5 shows that the contour of a region $R(p, L)$ is traced only counterclockwise between a p-entry point and the following p-exit point. The next theorem shows that there is an order principle for the p-entry and p-exit points, too.

Theorem 3.4.1.6 *Let p be in L_0, and let $v_1, v_1', v_2, v_2', \ldots, v_r, v_r'$ be the p-entry points and p-exit points as appearing in a bisecting chain K. Then the site p lies on the left of K, and $v_1, \ldots, v_r'$ are in counterclockwise order on the contour of $R(p, L)$. If K_1 and K_2 are two bisecting chains then the corresponding segments $(v_{1,1}, v_{r_1,1}')$ and $(v_{1,2}, v_{r_2,2}')$ of $\partial R(p, L)$ are disjoint.*

Proof: The first assertion follows from Lemma 3.3.3, 2), and Lemma 3.4.1.3. If, for two bisecting chains K_1 and K_2, the segments between the first p-entry point and the last p-exit point were not disjoint then one of them must be contained in the other one, because bisecting chains do not cross; see Figure 3.26. But then K_1 and K_2 are separated by a chain K that would fail to fulfill Lemma 3.3.3, 2). So does K_3.   □

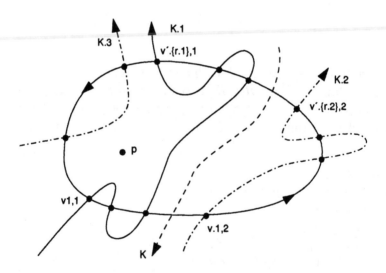

Figure 3.26: No chain can run like K_2 or K_3.

3.4.2   Finding the continuing segment

Suppose that during the execution of the algorithm *compute* of Section 3.2 a point v has been determined which is the endpoint of the chain segment b in $V(S)$. Assume that b is a $\{p, q\}$-borderline. From the values returned by the functions

L-endpoint and *R-endpoint* we know if v is contained in $V(L)$ ($e_L = true$), or in $V(R)$ ($e_R = true$), or in both.

If v is not contained in the augmenting curve Γ (i.e., if v-on-$\Gamma = false$) then the computation of the current bisecting chain must be continued. To this end, we have to find out which type of region in $V(S)$, L_0 or R_0, the point v belongs to. The site of v in $V(S)$ is computed by the following function.

```
1)      function site-of(v: point; p, q: site; e_L, e_R: boolean): site;
2)      var p̃, q̃: site;
3)      begin
4)          if e_L then          {v ∈ V(L)}
5)              if v is an inner point of a {p, p'}-borderline of V(L) then
6)                  p̃ := min(p, p')
7)              else             {v is vertex in V(L)}
8)                  p̃ := site stored in coordinate entry of v in Δ(L_0)
9)              end-if
10)         else                 {v in interior of R(p, L)}
11)             p̃ := p
12)         end-if;

13)         if e_R then ...      {analogously};

14)         if v ∈ D(p̃, q̃) then
15)             site-of := p̃
16)         else
17)             if v ∈ D(q̃, p̃) then
18)                 site-of := q̃
19)             else {v ∈ J(p̃, q̃)}
20)                 site-of := min(p̃, q̃)
21)             end-if
22)         end-if
23)     end-function
```

Lemma 3.4.2.1 *Let v be the endpoint of a maximal $\{p, q\}$-borderline b in $V(S)$, as determined in the previous step. Then*

$$v \in R(\text{site-of}(v, p, q, e_L, e_R), S)$$

Proof: Clearly, if $v \in R(\tilde{p}, L) \cap R(\tilde{q}, R)$ then v must belong either to $R(\tilde{p}, S)$ or to $R(\tilde{q}, S)$, depending on which side of $J(\tilde{p}, \tilde{q})$ v lies. This decision is made in lines 14–22 (to decide if a given point lies on the left of, on the right of, or on a bisecting curve, takes a further elementary operation; see Definition 3.4.3.1 below). In case v belongs to $J(\tilde{p}, \tilde{q})$, the smaller site wins (line 20). The site $\tilde{p}$ such that $v \in R(\tilde{p}, L)$ holds equals p if v is not a point of $V(L)$ (lines 10–11). If v belongs to $V(L)$ it is either an interior point of an edge, E, or a vertex. In the first case, the sites of the adjacent faces, p and p', are stored in the edge record of E in the representation $\Delta(L_0)$, which we still have access to, after termination of function L-endpoint in the previous step. In $V(L)$, v belongs to the region of the minimum of p, p' (line 6). In the second case, the coordinate entry of vertex v, which is stored in the record of each incident edge, already contains the name of $\tilde{p}$ (line 8).   □

Suppose that $site\text{-}of(v, p, q, e_L, e_R)$ belongs to an L_0-region. Then we have to determine the borderline b' of $J(L_0, R_0)$ radiating from v that is *counterclockwise next* to b. Assume that b' is a $\{p', q'\}$-borderline of $V(S)$. Then

*) $$b' \subset J(p', q') \cap R(p', L) \cap R(q', R).$$

Since we are in the non-degenerate case, b' does not coincide with one of the curves bordering $R(p', L)$ or $R(q', R)$. Conversely, assume that a segment b' of $J(p', q')$ radiating from v is contained in $R(p', L) \cap R(q', R)$, as shown in Figure 3.27. Then the points on the p'-side of b' belong to $R(p', L) \cap R(p', q') \cap R(q', R) \subset R(p', S)$. This can be verified by case analysis or by applying the transitivity property stated in Lemma 3.5.1.1 below. Similary, the points on the q'-side of and close to b' are contained in $R(q', S)$. Thus, b' is a $\{p', q'\}$-borderline in $V(S)$. *Consequently, one must determine the first segment b' in counterclockwise direction from b that has property* *).

Let b denote a bisecting curve segment incident with v. One can construct a function

$$counterclockwise\text{-}next(b, v)$$

that scans the regions of $V(L)$ and $V(R)$ at v simultaneously for the first *outgoing* curve segment b' in counterclockwise direction from b that fulfills property *); see Figure 3.28. The function is assumed to return the names of the adjacent sites of b', $p' = b'.L$ and $q' = b'.R$.

If b itself is an incoming bisecting chain segment, as above, then the counterclockwise next chain segment is automatically an outgoing one. In the simplest case, v is an inner point of an edge between p-land and p'-land in $V(L)$ and belongs to the interior of $R(q, R)$. Then the $\{p, q\}$-borderline b can only be followed by a $\{p', q\}$-borderline segment, and vice versa.

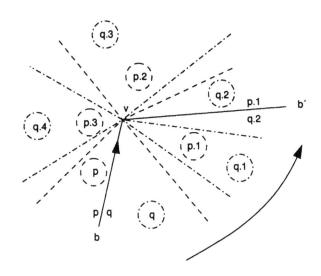

Figure 3.27: A segment $b' \subset J(p_1, q_2) \cap R(p_1, L) \cap R(q_2, R)$ must be a $\{p_1, q_2\}$-borderline in $V(S)$.

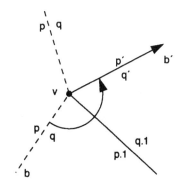

Figure 3.28: Scanning for b'.

The construction of function *counterclockwise-next* can be based on the "betweenness" operation: Given three curve segments, A, B, and C, that emanate from v, decide which of B, C comes first after A in counterclockwise direction. This decision is enabled by property E2 of Definition 3.4.3.1. It is clear that the number of operations required during execution of *counterclockwise-next* is of order $O(m)$, where m denotes the total number of edges of $V(L)$ and $V(R)$ between b and b', provided that the neighbor edges of b are accessible in $\Delta(L_0)$ and $\Delta(R_0)$ at no extra cost.

Now, determining the successor segment of b in a bisecting chain can be implemented as follows.

$$t := \textit{site-of}\,(v, p, q, e_L, e_R);$$
if $t \in L$ **then**
$$\qquad b' := \textit{counterclockwise-next}\,(b, v)$$
else $\{t \in R\}$
$$\qquad b' := \textit{clockwise-next}\,(b, v)$$
end-if;
$$p := b'.L;$$
$$q := b'.R;$$

Chew and Drysdale [14] have first pointed out that this simple method can be used for finding an initial chain segment at infinity, thereby unburdening the algorithm of maintaining convex hulls. In fact, after taking stereographic projection, the point $v = \infty$ can be treated as any vertex if the betweenness operation is extended to this case. Though we have not incorporated $v = \infty$ as a vertex into $\Delta(L_0)$ or $\Delta(R_0)$, the links between the infinite segments serve the same purpose; see Figure 3.2.

The very first chain segment b_∞ that goes out from Γ is computed in the following way. First, an arbitrary unbounded edge of $V(L_0), E$, is fixed (at least two such edges exist due to Lemma 2.7.2). Then the location of E with respect to the unbounded edges of $V(R_0)$ is determined, by scanning them in any order. After this synchronization is done, the same simultaneous scan procedure as above will find a first segment b_∞ within less than a full march around the pole. The statements

$$b_\infty := \textit{clockwise-next}\,(E, \infty);$$
$$p_\infty := b_\infty.L;$$
$$q_\infty := b_\infty.R;$$
$$e_L := \textit{true};$$

$e_R := true;$
$b := b_\infty;$
$p := b.L;$
$q := b.R;$

will serve as initialization, since the function searches for *outgoing* segments only. Each time the computation of a bisecting chain has been completed the segment outgoing from Γ clockwise next to b_∞ is found by

$$b_\infty := clockwise\text{-}next\ (b_\infty, \infty);$$

followed by the same assign statements as above, except the second and third. The very first values of p_∞ and q_∞ are stored and compared with the site of each newly computed initial chain segment, in order to assure termination of the algorithm. The position of current b_∞ is kept track of by means of two pointers, λ_∞ and ρ_∞, that are not changed as the current chain is computed. For the latter task, pointers λ and ρ are used.

3.4.3 The complete algorithm

Let *compute* denote the algorithm obtained by combining the modules presented in the previous subsections. While the bisecting chains are traced, in either representation, $\Delta(L_0)$ and $\Delta(R_0)$, the pointers to edge records, λ and ρ, are moved by the scan statements of the function *L-* (resp. *R-*) *endpoint* (line 22), and by the vertex scans performed by function *(counter-)clockwise-next*. Simultaneously, the bisecting chains are inserted into $\Delta(L_0)$ and $\Delta(R_0)$. This technique is well known from the Euclidean Voronoi diagram.

Now that $V(L_0)$ and $V(R_0)$ have been sewn up (using the bisecting chains as threads, and placing a stich wherever a chain segment ends) the final task consists in cutting off the excess material. The chains dissect the interior of Γ into finitely many domains each of which belongs either to the union of the L_0-regions, $\mathcal{L}$, or to $\mathcal{R}$, the union of all R_0-regions; cf. Figure 3.6. Those parts of $V(L_0)$ that are contained in an $\mathcal{R}$-domain must be removed, and similarly, all edges of $V(R_0)$ running through $\mathcal{L}$-regions. This can be done by tracing the bisecting chains again, and the augmenting curve Γ, and by disposing of all pointers to edge records in $\Delta(L_0)$ and $\Delta(R_0)$ that are no longer needed.

Definition 3.4.3.1 We call the following operations on a system $(S, \mathcal{J})$ of bisecting curves *elementary*.

E1) Given $J(p,q)$ and a point v, determine if $v \in D(p,q)$ holds.

E2) Given a point $v \in J(p,q) \cap J(r,s) \cap J(t,u)$ on the sphere and orientations of the curves, determine if $J(r,s)^+$ is prior to $J(t,u)^+$ in clockwise direction from $J(p,q)^+$, in a neighborhood of v. Here, J^+ denotes the curve segment outgoing from v.

E3) Given points $v \in J(p,q)$, $w \in J(p,r)$, and orientations, determine the first point of $J(p,r) |_{(w,\infty]}$ crossed by $J(p,q) |_{(v,\infty]}$.

E4) Given $J(p,q)$ with an orientation, and points v, w, x on $J(p,q)$, determine if v comes before w on $J(p,q) |_{(x,\infty)}$.

Note that E1 enables us to decide which of the sets $D(p,q), D(q,p), J(p,q)$ contains v. In E2 the curves have been identified with their mapped images under stereographic projection onto the sphere. For finite points v, the order of segments radiating from v is reversed under projection, which doesn't matter in the case of three segments. E2 also enables us to decide if two curve segments radiating from v coincide in a neighborhood of v. In E3, $v = \infty$ is returned if $J(p,r) |_{(w,\infty)} \cap J(p,q) |_{(v,\infty)} = \emptyset$.

By an $(S, \mathcal{J})$-*RAM* we mean a *real* Random Access Machine (see [52]) that can carry out each elementary operation on $(S, \mathcal{J})$ within one step, as an oracle call. Since the above operations E1–E4 can be formulated in terms of indices and real numbers, it is not implied that a (possibly space-consuming) description of the bisecting curves is stored in the machine. The orientation of a curve $J(p,q)$ can be represented by an ordered pair (p,q), indicating that $D(p,q)$ is on the left of $J(p,q)$.

Now we can formulate the main result of this section.

Theorem 3.4.3.2 *Let $(S_0, \mathcal{J}_0)$ be an admissible curve system with only proper crossings, and suppose that $S_0 = L_0 \cup R_0$ is an acyclic partition. Then $\Delta(L_0)$ and $\Delta(R_0)$ can be merged into $\Delta(S_0)$ within $O(| S_0 |)$ time and space on an $(S_0, \mathcal{J}_0)$-RAM.*

Proof: By induction on the number of chain segments, one shows that each bisecting chain is correctly computed by the algorithm *compute*. To this end, Theorem 3.4.1.5 and its counterpart valid for function *R-endpoint* are used, together with the correctness of the functions *(counter)-clockwise-next*.

Now let $n =| S_0 |$. Each of $V(L), V(R)$ being a planar map with $O(n)$ edges and vertices (Theorem 2.6.2), storing their representations needs not more than

$O(n)$ space. During the merge, edge records for the bisecting chain segments are generated; since such a segment is an edge of $V(S)$, the additional storage space needed is also of order n. This proves the space bound.

As to the time bound, each call of one of the functions *L-(R-)endpoint* and *(counter-)clockwise-next*, is related to a bisecting chain segment in a one-to-one way. Thus, only $O(n)$ function calls are made. The total amount of time spent on executing the functions *(counter-)clockwise-next* is charged to $V(L) \cup V(R)$ as follows. The scans performed on the edges of $V(L) \cup V(R)$ incident with a point v are either all in clockwise direction, or in counterclockwise direction, depending on the type of region in $V(S)$ the point v belongs to. Since bisecting chains do not cross, the sequences of consecutive edges traversed during each scan around v are mutually disjoint; see Figure 3.7. Therefore, the total number of edge accesses during all vertex scans is bounded by $O(n)$.

It remains to establish a bound for the number of edge visits during the contour scans performed by the functions *L-(R-)endpoint*. We may charge the first and the last edge access of each function call to the call itself. The additional edges visited during execution of line 22 of the algorithm are scanned in vane (i.e., without finding the cross-point v_L). By Theorem 3.4.1.6, the p-entry and p-exit points on the contour of $R(p, L_0)$ are visited by the chains in counterclockwise order. By Theorem 3.4.1.5, the sequence of edges between an entry point and the following exit point are scanned in counterclockwise order, without backtracking. Thus, no edge of $R(p, L)$ is scanned in vane twice. It follows that the total number of edge visits ever made in $V(L)$ is bounded by $O(n)$. The same holds for $V(R)$. It is routine to check that the sewing up and cutting off operations described at the beginning of this subsection can be carried out within the same time. Thereby, the time bound is established. $\qquad \Box$

3.5 The degenerate case

From now on we no longer impose restrictions on how two bisecting curves of the underlying curve system intersect. This gives rise to several problems. First, when the endpoint of a bisecting chain segment $b \in J(p, q)$ in $V(L \cup \{q\})$ is to be determined, we must disregard those points of $\partial R(p, L)$ the segment b can run through without loosing its $\{p, q\}$-borderline status; see Figure 3.29. This problem will be taken care of by defining what a cross-point is; see Subsection 3.5.2. In addition, one point of $\partial R(p, L)$ can induce many points of the planar map $V(S)$, all of which can belong to the edge cycle around $R(p, L)$, see Figure

3.30. Nevertheless, such induced points are still *ordered* on the contour of $R(p, L)$. In the representation $\Delta(L_0)$ of $V(L_0)$ there are no direct links between different points that are induced by the same point v of $\partial R(p, L)$. Thus, when the contour of $R(p, L)$ is traced and when an induced point (v, B) is encountered, we have only *partial information* on the neighborhood of v in $V(L)$. The exact amount of information associated with (v, B) is described by the following lemma.

Definition 3.5.1 Let U be an admissible neighborhood of $v \in V(S)$, and let (v, B) be a point induced by v. Then

$$\text{sites}(v, B) := \{q \in S; B \text{ contains a } q\text{-borderline}\},$$
$$\text{sites}(v) := \bigcup_{\substack{(v, B) \text{ induced} \\ \text{by } v}} \text{sites}(v, B).$$

Clearly, if $v \in V(S)$ then $U \cap V(\text{sites}(v)) = U \cap V(S)$ holds. This property of locality carries over to induced points.

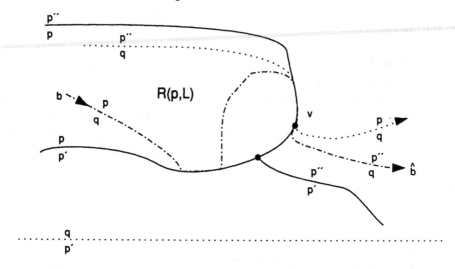

Figure 3.29: Bisecting chain segment b does not end before point v, if $p < q, p''$.

Lemma 3.5.2 Let U be an admissible neighborhood of $v \in V(S)$, let (v, B) be induced by v, and let $p_\mu = \min(\text{sites}(v))$. Then for each $q \in \text{sites}(v, B)$ we have

$$U \cap R(q, \text{sites}(v, B)) = U \cap R(q, S), \qquad \text{if} \quad q \neq p_\mu.$$
$$U \cap R(p_\mu, \text{sites}(v, B)) = U \cap \left(R(p_\mu, S) \cup \bigcup_{\substack{t \in \text{sites}(v) \\ t \notin \text{sites}(v, B)}} R(t, S) \right)$$

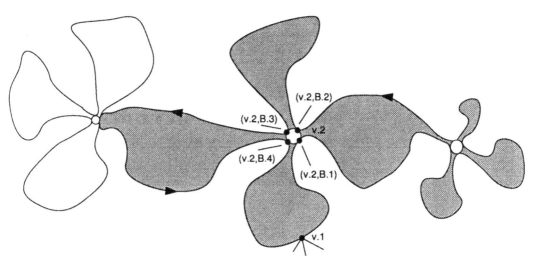

Figure 3.30: Multiple points on a region contour.

Therefore,

$$\bigcup_{\substack{(v,B) \ induced \\ by \ v}} U \cap V(sites(v,B)) = U \cap V(S).$$

Proof: If a point z of $R(t,S)$, where $t \notin sites(v,B)$, were contained in a region $R(q, sites(v,B))$, $q \neq p_\mu$, then more than one piece of U would belong to this region, in contradiction to Theorem 2.3.5. Thus, $z \in R(p_\mu, (sites(v,B)))$ holds, see Figure 3.31.   □

In the following, we are making use of Lemma 3.5.2 without explicit mention.

3.5.1   Local separation of curves

In this subsection a result is derived that will prove a handy tool because it frees us from considering all special cases arising from bisecting curves that coincide in a neighborhood of a given point.

First, we prove that condition 2 B) of the definition of an admissible curve system (2.1.2) can actually be replaced by a (formally) weaker property. The short proof of Case 2 is due to St. Meiser [44].

Lemma 3.5.1.1 *Let $(S, \mathcal{J})$ be a system of bisecting curves. Then the following assertions are equivalent.*

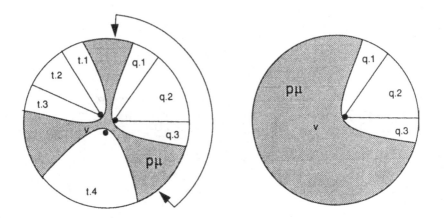

Figure 3.31: Neighborhoods of v in $V(S)$ and in $V(\text{sites}(v, B))$.

1. *If p, q and r are pairwise different sites of S then $R(p,q) \cap R(q,r) \subseteq R(p,r)$ holds. (Transitivity)*

2. *For each subset $S' \subseteq S$ of cardinality 3 we have*

$$\Re^2 = \bigcup_{p \in S'} R(p, S').$$

3. *Property 2) holds for an arbitrary non-empty subset S' of S.*

Proof: 3) trivially implies 2).
2) $\Longrightarrow$ 1) : Let z be contained in $R(p,q) \cap R(q,r)$. By 2), there must be a site t in $S' := \{p, q, r\}$ such that $z \in R(t, S')$. If $t = p$ then $z \in R(p, S') \subseteq R(p, r)$, as stated. Otherwise, $z \in R(q, S') \subseteq R(q, p)$ would contradict $z \in R(p, q)$, and $z \in R(r, S') \subseteq R(r, q)$ would contradict $z \in R(q, r)$.
1) $\Longrightarrow$ 3) : By induction on $|S'|$. If S' is of size ≤ 2, then the assertion is immediate. The case where $|S'| = 3$ follows directly from 1). Assume that $|S'| \geq 4$, and let z be a point in the plane. By induction hypothesis, to each $p \in S'$ there exists a site $c(p) \neq p$ such that $z \in R(c(p), S' - \{p\})$ holds.
Case 1: $c(v) = c(w)$. Then

$$\begin{aligned} z \ &\in \ R(c(v), S' - \{v\}) \cap R(c(v), S' - \{w\}) \\ &\subset \ R(c(v), S' - \{v\}) \cap R(c(v), v) = R(c(v), S'). \end{aligned}$$

Case 2: The mapping c is injective. Let p, v, w be such that the set $\{p, c(p), v, w\}$ is of size 4. Since $c(v) \neq c(w)$, one of $c(v), c(w)$—say $c(v)$—is different from p.

Because of $c(v) \neq c(p)$ we obtain the contradiction

$$z \in R(c(p), S' - \{p\}) \subseteq R(c(p), c(v))$$
$$z \in R(c(v), S' - \{v\}) \subseteq R(c(v), c(p)).$$

$\square$

Note that the first property in the lemma corresponds to the transitivity of $<$ in concrete metrics. Now we show how to separate curves that coincide in the neighborhood of a given point

Theorem 3.5.1.2 *Let $(S, \mathcal{J})$ be an admissible curve system, and let v be a point in the plane. In a suitable neighborhood U of v, the curves of $\mathcal{J}$ passing v can be deformed in such a way that the resulting system $(\tilde{S}, \tilde{\mathcal{J}})$ is admissible and has the following properties.*

1. *If $v \in J(p, q) \cap J(r, s)$ then v is the only point of intersection of the deformed curves, $\tilde{\mathcal{J}}(p, q)$ and $\tilde{\mathcal{J}}(r, s)$, inside U.*

2. *For each non-empty $T \subseteq S$ the cyclical sequence of borderlines radiating from v is the same in $V(T)$ as in $V(\tilde{T})$.*

Here S and $\tilde{S}$ are equal as sets of indices; the sites in the plane may have to be chosen differently. The order of borderlines has been addressed in Theorem 2.3.5; recall that their order is uniquely determined by the order of the Voronoi regions round v, and vice versa.

Proof: Let U be a neighborhood of v as in Lemma 2.3.2. Assume that there are two or more curves of $\mathcal{J}$ that have an arc α in common which extends from v to ∂U (endpoints not included). We have to separate these curves by spreading them out like the wires of a cable, without touching the neighbor curves of α; see Figure 3.32. To prove the theorem, it is sufficient to show how to separate the wires of *one* cable incident with v.

By D_l (resp. D_r) we denote the area of U on the left (resp. on the right) of and close to α. A biscecting curve $J(p, q)$ that runs through α is denoted by $p \mid q$ iff $D_l \subset D(p, q)$ (and consequently, $D_r \subset D(q, p)$) holds, and by $q \mid p$, otherwise; note that no ambiguity can arise since bisecting curves are simple.

Now assume that $J(p, q)$ and $J(p, r)$ are both passing through α. In order to separate them, we have to decide which one comes first in left-to-right order, as seen from v. Due the property 2), this order must agree with the situation at v in

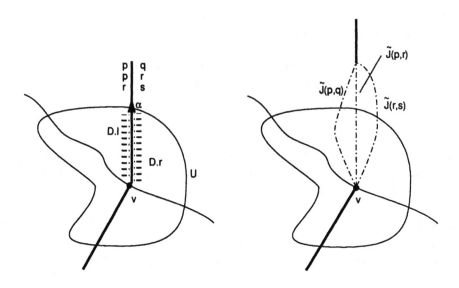

Figure 3.32: Separation of curve segments.

$V(\{p,q,r\})$. Here α can induce one or two borderlines, depending on $J(q,r)$ and on the order relations between p, q, and r. A complete case analysis is displayed in Figure 3.33. On the right hand side the correct order of curves is shown which turns out to be uniquely determined in each case; borderlines are drawn bold, and Voronoi regions are marked by encircling site labels.

Note that in case 1.3 the relations $r < p < q$ are in fact impossible. For, $p < q$ would imply

$$\alpha \subset J(p,q) \subset R(p,q),$$

hence, because of $\alpha \subset D(q,r)$,

$$\alpha \subset R(p,\{p,q,r\}) \subset R(p,r)$$

which contradicts $\alpha \subset J(r,p) \subset R(r,p)$ if $r < p$.

In case 3, D_l must belong to r-land since it cannot belong to p-land nor to q-land. Similary, D_r is contained in q-land. Hence, $r|q$ must be in α.

Now the intended order of curves is defined as follows.

Definition 3.5.1.3 Let $p \mid q$ and $p \mid r$ (resp. $q \mid p$ and $r \mid p$) be in α.

$$\left.\begin{array}{l} p \mid q \longrightarrow p \mid r \ : \ \Longleftrightarrow \\ r \mid p \longrightarrow q \mid p \ : \ \Longleftrightarrow \end{array}\right\} \ \alpha \text{ induces a } \{p,q\}\text{-borderline in } V(\{p,q,r\})$$

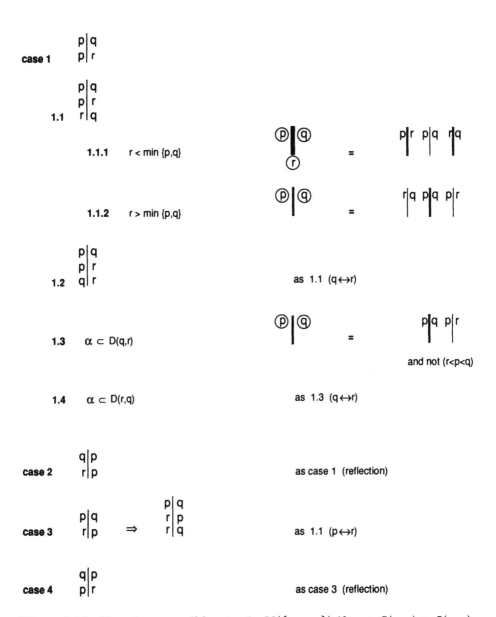

Figure 3.33: Situations possible at α in $V(\{p,q,r\})$ if $\alpha \subset J(p,q) \cap J(p,r)$.

Obviously, the second line follows from the first by applying reflection. An investigation of Figure 3.33 immediately shows that this definition captures the correct order.

Claim 1 If $J(p,q)$ and $J(p,r)$ contain α then they are comparable in the transitive closure of $\longrightarrow$, restricted to pairs of sites in $\{p,q,r\}$, and the correct order of separation is given by the direction of arrows.

Here at most two arrows are necessary to relate $J(p,q)$ to $J(p,r)$; this happens in case 3 and case 4. Claim 1 assures us that the above definition is necessary in order to fulfill property 2) of the theorem. The problem is in proving that relation $\longrightarrow$ can in fact be extended to an order relation for all sites in S; there could be cycles in $\longrightarrow$ arising from other site sets $\{p,q,s\},\{q,r,s\},\ldots$ which make a consistent global ordering impossible.

Claim 2 If $\quad p\,|\,q \longrightarrow p\,|\,r \longrightarrow p\,|\,s \quad$ then $\quad p\,|\,q \longrightarrow p\,|\,s$.
$\qquad\quad$ If $\quad s\,|\,p \longrightarrow r\,|\,p \longrightarrow q\,|\,p \quad$ then $\quad s\,|\,p \longrightarrow q\,|\,p$.

Proof: The second assertion follows from the first by reflection. For $\{a,b,c\} \subseteq T$, some T, let abc denote the situation where we have $D_l \subset R(a,T), \alpha \subset R(b,T)$, and $D_r \subset R(c,T)$. If we assume $p\,|\,q \longrightarrow p\,|\,r$ and $p\,|\,r \longrightarrow p\,|\,s$ then the following situations are possible.

$$\text{In } V(\{p,q,r\}): \quad ppq, \quad pqq, \quad pqr$$

$$\text{In } V(\{p,r,s\}): \quad ppr, \quad prr, \quad prs$$

Using $R(p,\{p,q,r\}) \cap R(r,\{p,r,s\}) = \emptyset$ and inclusions like

$$R(q,\{p,q,r\}) \cap R(r,\{p,r,s\}) \ \subset \ R(q,r) \cap R(r,s) \subset R(q,s)$$
$$\subset \ R(q,\{p,q,r,s\})$$

which follow by transitivity (Lemma 3.5.1.1, 1)), it is easy to check that only the following situations can result from the above.

$$\text{In } V(\{p,q,r,s\}): \quad ppq, \quad pqq, \quad pqr, \quad pqs$$

Hence, α induces a $\{p,q\}$-borderline in $V(\{p,q,s\})$, that is $p\,|\,q \longrightarrow p\,|\,s$ holds. $\square$

Now the key observation is the following.

Claim 3

$$\text{If} \quad p \mid q \longrightarrow p \mid r \quad \text{then} \quad (p < q \Longrightarrow p < r).$$
$$\text{If} \quad r \mid p \longrightarrow q \mid p \quad \text{then} \quad (r < p \Longrightarrow q < p).$$

The proof is by case analysis, guided by Figure 3.33. Note that again the second line follows from the first by reflection, because the right hand side implications are equivalent.

Claim 4 *Relation* $\longrightarrow$ *is acyclic.*

Proof: Otherwise, let C be a cycle of minimum length. Due to Claim 3, we may assume that $p < q$ holds for each term $p \mid q$ that occurs in C (should always $q < p$ be true we could apply reflection). Because of Claim 2 and the supposed minimality of C, transitions of type

$$w \mid q \longrightarrow p \mid q, \qquad p \mid q \longrightarrow p \mid r$$

must interchange in C; in particular, C is of even length. For each transition of type $p \mid q \longrightarrow p \mid r$ in C the arc α either contains $r \mid q$, or is contained in $D(q, r)$. This follows by checking up on the remaining cases shown in Figure 3.33; note that only those situations need be examined where α induces *one* borderline of $V(\{p, q, r\})$, since $p < q$ and $p < r$ hold! Hence, we obtain

$$p \mid q \longrightarrow p \mid r \text{ in } C \Longrightarrow D_r \subset D(q, r).$$

Now suppose that C is the sequence of transitions

$$p_i \mid q_i \longrightarrow p_{i+1} \mid q_i \longrightarrow p_{i+1} \mid q_{i+1}, \qquad 1 \le i \le m - 1,$$

where $p_m = p_1$ and $q_m = q_1$. Then

$$D_r \subset \bigcap_{i=1}^{m-2} D(q_i, q_{i+1}) \cap D(q_{m-1}, q_1),$$

which is impossible because the points of D_r would then not be contained in any region of the Voronoi diagram $V(\{q_1, q_2, \ldots, q_{m-1}\})$. □

Since relation $\longrightarrow$ is acyclic it can be embedded in a linear order which is afterwards extended in an arbitrary way to all those curves passing through α that do not belong to the domain of $\longrightarrow$. Let $(\tilde{S}, \tilde{\mathcal{J}})$ denote the curve system where the curves of $\mathcal{J}$ formerly running through α have been bent in an appropriate way, according to the order just defined.

Claim 5 For each non-empty set $T \subset S$, the regions $R(p, \widetilde{T})$ form a partition of the plane.

Proof: Due to Lemma 3.5.1.1 we need only prove this if $T = \{p, q, r\}$ is of size 3. If none, or only one, of the associated bisecting curves of $\mathcal{J}$ is passing α, the assertion follows immediately (in the latter case the bent curve in $\widetilde{\mathcal{J}}$ does not interfere with its two companions).

Assume that two or three curves of $\mathcal{J}$ associated with T contain α. Then Claim 1 guarantees that the neighborhood of v looks the same in $V(T)$ as in $V(\widetilde{T})$, so that each point is contained in a Voronoi region.   □

It is also clear that we have not caused a region $R(p, \widetilde{T})$ to be disconnected, if $|T| = 3$. Hence, the curve system of T in $\widetilde{\mathcal{J}}$ is admissible and fulfills property 2) of the theorem. Now let $T \subseteq S$ be of arbitrary size ≥ 4. Let $p_1, p_2, \ldots, p_m$ denote the sites of the regions of $V(\widetilde{T})$ as they now appear where α has been before, see Figure 3.34.

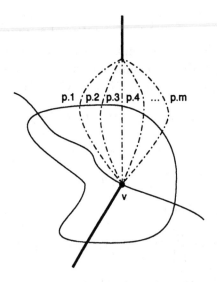

Figure 3.34: Not a possible neighborhood of v in $V(\widetilde{T})$.

Assume that $m \geq 4$. Let $Q_1 = \{p_1, p_2, p_3\}$ and $Q_2 = \{p_2, p_3, p_4\}$. Then in $V(\widetilde{Q_1})$ (resp. $V(\widetilde{Q_2})$) the regions of p_1, p_2, p_3 (resp. p_2, p_3, p_4) appear in the same order. Since this must be the original order in $V(Q_1)$ and $V(Q_2)$, we conclude $p_2 < p_1, p_3$, and $p_3 < p_2, p_4$, which is a contradiction. Assume $m = 3$. We have $D_l \subset R(p_1, T)$ and $D_r \subset R(p_3, T)$ because the position of the points in D_l and D_r relative to the wires in α has not changed. If α were contained in a region $R(p, T)$ where $p \neq p_2$ then $p \neq p_1$ or $p \neq p_3$. In the first case, α would be a $\{p, p_1\}$-borderline in $V(T)$, so we would have $p_1 \mid p \longrightarrow p_1 \mid p_2$, in contradiction to Figure 3.34.

This implies that the regions in $V(\widetilde{T})$ are still pathwise connected, and that property 2) holds for T. Thus, the system $(\widetilde{S}, \widetilde{\mathcal{J}})$ is admissible, fulfills 2), and the wires of cable α are separated now.

This completes the proof of Theorem 3.5.1.2. □

Thanks to this theorem, which applies to augmented curve systems as well, we can w.l.o.g. *assume that in a neighborhood of a given point, v, any two bisecting curves intersect only in v, whenever we want to derive results that depend only on the order of borderlines and regions.* The algorithm must work on the original curves. But if only a bounded number of curve segments radiating from a point are involved (during execution of function *clockwise-next*, for example) the algorithm can compute their relative order with respect to $\rightarrow$ *adhoc*, and perform as it would with a non-degenerate system.

The curve system $(\widetilde{S}, \widetilde{\mathcal{J}})$ will be called a *normalization of* $(S, \mathcal{J})$ *at* v.

Clearly, the way two wires are separated is the same at each point v of a cable α because it depends on the global order $<$ on the set of sites, S. If we apply Theorem 3.5.1.2 to each point of $V(S)$ that is not an endpoint of a connected component of an intersection of curves we arrive at a new family of admissible curves that do no longer share segments. The Voronoi diagrams that can be constructed from the subfamilies have not been changed, up to deformations. But the new regions can have only *isolated* cut-points.

3.5.2 Cross-points

When the endpoint of a bisecting chain segment $b \subset J(p, q)$ is to be determined the contour of $R(p, L)$ must be scanned for such induced points that terminate the $\{p, q\}$-borderline status of b.

Definition 3.5.2.1 Let (v, B) be an induced point of $V(L)$, let $p \in \text{sites}(v, B)$ and $q \in R = S - L$. Then (v, B) is called a *cross-point* or $J(p, q)$ iff $v \in J(p, q)$, and iff exactly one of the two curve segments of $J(p, q)$ radiating from v is a $\{p, q\}$-borderline with respect to $\text{sites}(v, B) \cup \{q\}$, in a neighborhood of v. This one is called the *active* segment, the other one is called *dead*.

Each cross-point (v, B) of $J(p, q)$ belongs to the edge cycle around $R(p, L)$. For, the neighbor of the p-region adjacent to the active segment of $J(p, q)$ in

$V(\text{sites}(v, B) \cup \{q\})$ must be a site p' different from q, or the other segment of $J(p, q)$ would also be active. It is important to realize that *the active segment need not be a $\{p, q\}$-borderline in $V(\text{sites}(v) \cup \{q\})$*, if more than one point of $V(L)$ is induced by v; see Figure 3.35. The dead segment, however, remains dead with respect to each set of sites that includes $\text{sites}(v, B) \cup \{q\}$, *a fortiori*. Thus, cross-points are the right points the contour of $R(p, L)$ must be scanned for. In the following, it is assumed that (v, B) is an induced point of $V(L)$, and that $p \in \text{sites}(v, B)$ and $q \in R$ hold.

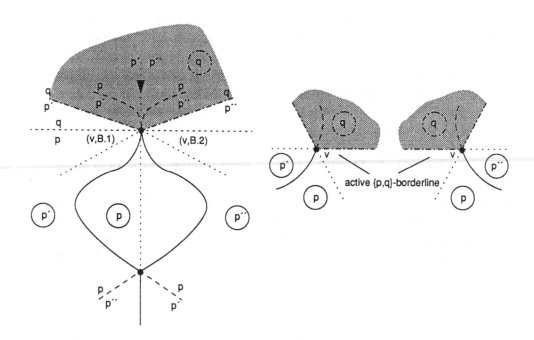

Figure 3.35: $V(\text{sites}(v) \cup \{q\})$, $V(\text{sites}(v, B_1) \cup \{q\})$, and $V(\text{sites}(v, B_2) \cup \{q\})$. Each of the active parts of $J(p, q)$ in the latter two diagrams is dead in the first one. We have $p < p', p''$.

Using normalization (Theorem 3.5.1.2) we can relate cross-points according to the above Definiton to the "proper" cross-points of the non-degenerate case in the following way.

Lemma 3.5.2.2 *The induced point (v, B) is a cross-point of $J(p, q)$ iff, in a normalization at v, $\widetilde{J}(p, q)$ properly crosses the contour of the region $R(p, \widetilde{\text{sites}}(v, B))$ at v.*

The proof is easy. Note that the region of p is represented exactly once at the induced point (v, B). Clearly, the segment of $\widetilde{J}(p, q)$ contained herein corresponds to the active piece of $J(p, q)$; see Figure 3.36. The following lemmata can be directly obtained by normalization.

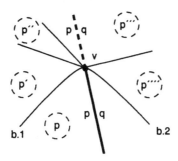

Figure 3.36: A proper cross-point in $V(\text{sites}(v, B))$.

Lemma 3.5.2.3 *In the map $V(L)$ at most two points induced by v can be cross-points of $J(p, q)$. In this case, $p = \min(\text{sites}(v))$ holds, and none of the two segments of $J(p, q)$ radiating from v is a $\{p, q\}$-borderline in $V(L \cup \{q\})$.*

This case is illustrated by Figure 3.35.

Lemma 3.5.2.4 *The endpoint of a maximal $\{p, q\}$-borderline b in $V(L \cup \{q\})$ in a given direction is the first point v of $J(p, q)$ such that a cross-point (v, B) of $J(p, q)$ exists in $V(L)$; (v, B) is uniquely determined among the points induced by v.*

The simplest cross-points are those where $|B| = 2$ holds. Such points arise from each inner point of a $\{p, p'\}$-borderline in $V(L)$. If (v, B) is a cross-point of $J(p, q)$ then $J(p, p')$ and $J(p, q)$ are said to *cross at v*. This notion is symmetric in $J(p, p')$ and $J(p, q)$ because (v, B) is a cross-point of $J(p, q)$ iff v induces a vertex in $V(\{p, p', q\})$. In particular, if $J(p, p')$ and $J(p, q)$ *cross at v then the curve $J(p', q)$ must pass through v, too.* This is an important property abstract Voronoi diagrams share with most concrete diagrams. In the non-degenerate case it can be easily derived from Definition 2.1.2.

The order of cross-points of $J(p, q)$ is the same on $J(p, q)$ as on the contour of $R(p, L)$. Indeed, we can apply Lemma 3.4.1.3 after "thickening" the cut-points of $R(p, L)$ that remain in a global normalisation, and after detaching $J(p, q)$ where it touches $\partial R(p, L)$ without crossing it; this does not destroy the connectedness of $R(p, L) \cup R(p, q)$. The same applies to the bisecting chains.

At the end of this subsection we derive a restriction on the number of cross-points of two bisecting curves that belong to the same site, p.

Lemma 3.5.2.5 *Let p, q, t be three different sites of S_0. Then $J(p, q)$ and $J(p, t)$ cross at most twice.*

Proof: Let $S' = \{p, q, t, \infty\}$. The augmented diagram $V(S')$ is a planar map with exactly 4 faces. By the Euler Formula (cf. the proof of Lemma 1.1.1), it follows that $2v + 4 = 2e \geq 3v$, that is $v \leq 4$. At least two vertices are located on the augmenting curve Γ, since $V(S')$ is biconnected (Lemma 2.7.2). Therefore, there can be at most two finite vertices. The assertion follows because each crossing induces a vertex.   □

The above restriction on the number of cross-points of two bisecting curves $J(p, q), J(p, t)$, is essentially due to the *connectedness* of the Voronoi regions required in Definition 2.1.2. However, there is *no* restriction implied on the number of times two *arbitrary* bisecting curves can cross; see Figure 3.37.

One can show that the converse of Lemma 3.5.2.5 also holds true: if any two p-bisectors cross at most twice and never in such a way that a clockwise oriented cycle results, then all Voronoi regions are connected. Together with Lemma 3.5.1.1, this allows to test a given curve system for admissibility *by checking only the subsets of S of size 3*; see [35]. This reduces the exponential complexity of Definition 2.1.2 to cubic complexity.

3.5.3   The modified algorithm

In the degenerate case, the functions introduced in Section 3.4 must work on induced points, rather than on points (to avoid type mismatch, it is convenient to consider an "ordinary" point v, that is not contained in a Voronoi diagram, an induced point $(v, \emptyset)$). For example

$$clockwise\text{-}next(b, (v, B_L), (v, B_R))$$

scans the edges of $B_L \cup B_R$ simultaneously for the clockwise first segment $b' \subset J(p', q')$ outgoing from v after b, that induces a $\{p', q'\}$-borderline with respect to sites $(v, B_L) \cup$ sites(v, B_R). The relative local order of a bounded number of bisector segments some of which may locally coincide can be determined by $O(1)$

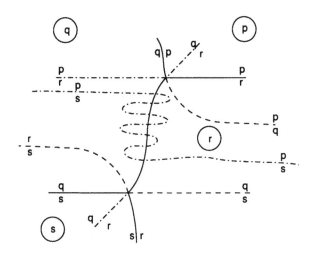

Figure 3.37: $J(p,s)$ and $J(q,r)$ may cross arbitrarily often.

elementary operations; see the remark at the end of Subsection 3.5.1. Similary, testing whether or not a vertex encountered during a contour scan is a cross-point reduces to the non-degenerate case; see the results of Subsection 3.5.2.

All these changes are of a more technical nature. With the notion of cross-points, the determination of endpoints is not different from the non-degenerate case. We shall concentrate on an *essential* difference between the degenerate and the non-degenerate case, caused by a difficulty in computing continuing chain segments. This difficulty can only arise if a region contains cut-points, that is if bisecting curves $J(p,q)$, $J(p,r)$ *touch at their p-sides*.

Example: In Figure 3.38 an admissible curve system is shown for the site set $S_0 = L_0 \cup R_0$, where $L_0 = \{p, p', p''\}, R_0 = \{q, q'\}$ and $p = \min(S_0)$. There are two bisecting chains in $J(L_0, R_0)$, K_1 and K_2, that consist of chain segments $p'' \mid q'$, $p \mid q'$, $p' \mid q'$, and $p' \mid q$, $p \mid q$, correspondingly. The curve system depicted in Figure 3.39 results from the former by squeezing the curves together such that all the points of intersection shown in Figure 3.38 now become the same point, v. Since $p = \min(S)$, the point v belongs to $R(p, S)$. Therefore, an incoming chain segment ending at v must be continued by the chain segment *counterclockwise* next to it. Thus, K_1 and K_2 are still the correct bisecting chains in the degenerate curve system. The chains, and the two points induced by v on the contour of $R(p, L)$, are shown in Figure 3.40.

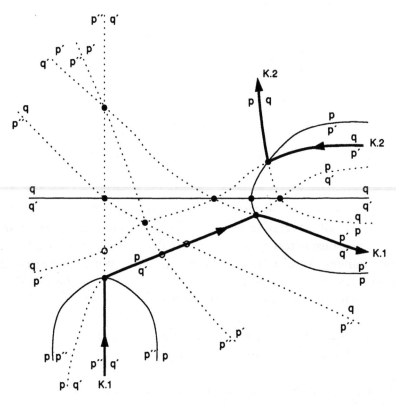

Figure 3.38: An admissible curve system with bisecting chains K_1 and K_2.

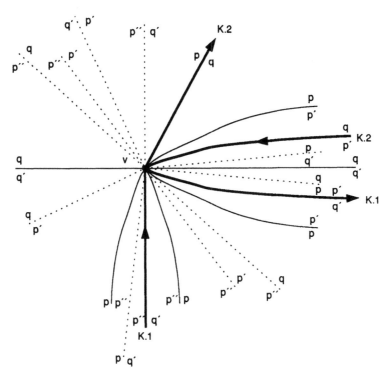

Figure 3.39: The system of Figure 3.38 contracted at v.

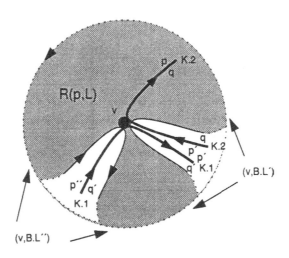

Figure 3.40: The region $R(p, L)$, as trespassed by the bisecting chains K_1 and K_2. The dotted circle is the augmenting curve, Γ.

Now assume that (v, B_L'') and (v, B_R), the only point of $V(R)$ induced by v, have been determined as endpoints of the chain segment $p'' \mid q'$ in $V(L)$ and $V(R)$, correspondingly. Then the next step is calling the function

$$\textit{counterclockwise-next}(p'' \mid q', (v, B_L''), (v, B_R))$$

that scans only the borderlines in $B_L'' \cup B_R$ (note that we cannot do better at this moment, for lack of knowledge of the existence of (v, B_L')). As illustrated by Figure 3.41, the continuing segment returned will be the $p \mid q$-segment which is *not* the correct continuation of K_1 in $V(S)$.

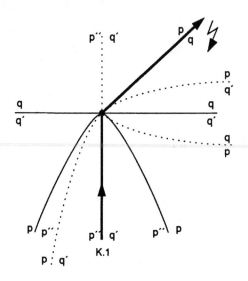

Figure 3.41: In $V(\text{sites}(v, B_L'') \cup R)$, K_1 is continued by the $p \mid q$-chain segment!

However, there is a remedy for this fault. As soon as the contour of $R(p, L)$ is scanned in counterclockwise order, the other point induced by $v, (v, B_L')$, will be encountered *before* the first cross-point of the $p \mid q$-segment. Then, special action can be taken: in order to detect the correct continuation of K_1, namely $p' \mid q'$, it is now necessary to scan (v, B_L') and (v, B_R) for the first outgoing chain segment counterclockwise next to the $p'' \mid q'$-segment. This in turn requires to backtrack the pointer of $\Delta(R), \rho$, from its position near the $p \mid q$-borderline. As we will see, performance problems can be avoided by a careful implementation.

In order to report such multiple points on a region contour, the functions L-$(R$-$)$ *endpoint* are modified as follows. Whenever the contour of $R(p, L)$ is scanned during execution of

$$L\text{-endpoint}(p, q, (v, B_L), e_L, T_L)$$

(lines 22-23 of the algorithm in Subsection 3.4.1) then *the first point* (v', B_L') *on the contour in counterclockwise direction after* (v, B_L) *is reported such that* (v', B_L') *is a cross-point of* $J(p, q) \mid_{(v, \infty)}$ *or* $v' = v$.

Now we discuss how the modified functions can be used for correctly determining the continuing chain segment, even if multiple vertices occur.

Assume that v is endpoint of a bisecting chain segment $b_0 \subset J(p_0, q_0)$ in $V(S)$. With respect to Theorem 3.5.1.2 we shall assume that in a neighborhood of v no two bisecting curves intersect, except at v. Suppose that (v, B_L) and (v, B_R) are the unique cross-points of $J(p_0, q_0)$ in $V(L)$ and $V(R)$. Let p_m be the site of v in $V(S)$, and assume $p_m \in L$. Let $R_1 = \text{sites}(v, B_R)$, for short.

We first show how to compute the continuation, b_1, *of* b_0 *in* $V(L \cup R_1)$. *In a second phase, the correct continuation in* $V(S)$, b_2, *is determined.*

Phase 1 (The computation of b_1) The segment

$$b := \text{counterclockwise-next } (b_0, (v, B_L), (v, B_R))$$

is the correct successor of b_0 in $V(\text{sites}(v, B_L) \cup R_1)$.

Claim 1 b_1 comes before b in counterclockwise order from b_0 (see Figure 3.42).

Proof: The area between b_0 and b_1 belongs to R_1-regions of $V(L \cup R_1)$. These do not shrink, as L is decreased to $\text{sites}(v, B_L)$. □

Claim 2 If the adjacent L-site, $b_1.L$, of b_1 belongs to $\text{sites}(v, B_L)$ then $b_1 = b$. This holds in particular true if (v, B_L) is the only point of $V(L)$ induced by v.

Proof: Claim 1 and the definition of b. □

Assume that b is a $\{p, q\}$-borderline w.r.t. $\text{sites}(v, B_L) \cup R_1$. If $p \neq p_m$ then $b = b_1$ because the other points of $V(L)$ induced by v do not interfere with b (note that, since $v \in R(p_m, S)$, p_m-land must lie on the left hand side of the chain b_0, b in $V(\text{sites}(v, B_L) \cup R_1)$, due to Lemma 3.3.2, so b cannot be rotated too far). Suppose that $p = p_m$. Next,

$$(v_L', B_L') := L\text{-endpoint}(p_m, q, (v, B_L), \text{true}, T_L)$$

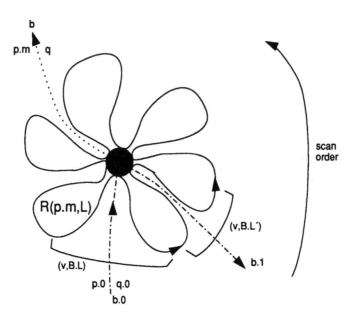

Figure 3.42: Continuations, b and b_1, of b_0 in $V(\text{sites}(v, B_L) \cup R_1)$ and $V(L \cup R_1)$.

is executed. Two cases arise. If $v_L' \neq v$ then b must be equal to b_1. Otherwise, the situation would have to look as depicted in Figure 3.43, due to Claim 1 and Claim 2, contradicting Lemma 3.4.1.3. In the second case, $v_L' = v$. Now we know that v is a cut-point of $R(p_m, L)$, and that the first point induced by v after (v, B_L) has been encountered, due to the modification of function L-endpoint.

We want to resume the simultaneous edge scan, in order to detect b_1. By the last contour scan, the pointer of $\Delta(L_0)$, λ, has been moved to the first (p_m)-borderline, E, of B_L'. The pointer of $\Delta(R_0)$, ρ, however has advanced as far as to b during the previous call of $counterclockwise\text{-}next$, and must therefore be moved back to the position of E. On the way, many edges of B_R may be traversed; *in order to avoid future backtrack in the edge "interval" of B_R between the positions of E and b, all these edges are marked with "$p_m \mid q$"*, see Figure 3.44. Then

$$b := counterclockwise\text{-}next(E, (v, B_L'), (v, B_R))$$

is executed. This time, b is either equal to b_1, if b_1 lies between the p_m-borderlines of B_L', as shown in Figure 3.44, or again b is the continuation of b_0 in $V(\text{sites}(v, B_L) \cup \text{sites}(v, B_R) \cup R_1)$. *But this time, the edges of B_R need not be scanned as far as to b, because the marks "$p_m \mid q$" give the correct information that this segment is ahead, and that it is the continuation of b_0 with respect to R_1 and the sites at v in*

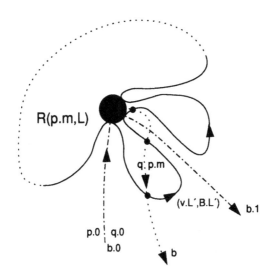

Figure 3.43: This course of b would disconnect $R(p_m, L \cup \{q\})$.

$V(L)$ so far encountered. Now *L-endpoint* and *counterclockwise-next* are executed alternately, until b_1 is detected, with only counterclockwise scan operations.

For this to work, the function *counterclockwise-next* must be modified such that the execution of

$$b := counterclockwise\text{-}next\ (E, (v, B_L'), (v, B_R))$$

stops as soon as a p_m-edge of B_L' has been traversed towards its p_m-side, provided that the following edge of B_R is marked with "$p_m \mid x$", some x, and that the inscription read is returned. Here p_m is the site stored in each edge record of B_L' with the coordinates of v, i.e. the site whose region contains v.

By the above algorithm the continuation b_1 of b_0 in $V(L \cup sites(v, B_R))$ has been determined. If b_1 is a p_m-borderline, then $b_1 = b$, and also the endpoint, (v_L', B_L'), of b_1 in $V(L \cup R_1)$ has been found on the contour of $R(p, L)$ (as returned by the last call of *L-endpoint*).

Phase 2 Now we turn to computing b_2, the correct continuation of b_0 in $V(S)$.

Claim 3 b_2 comes after b_1 in counterclockwise direction from b_0.

The proof is as of Claim 1. Let q_m be the site in R such that $v \in R(q_m, R)$. Trivially, if $b_2 \neq b_1$, then more than one point of $V(R)$ is induced by v, and v is a cut-point of $R(q_m, R)$.

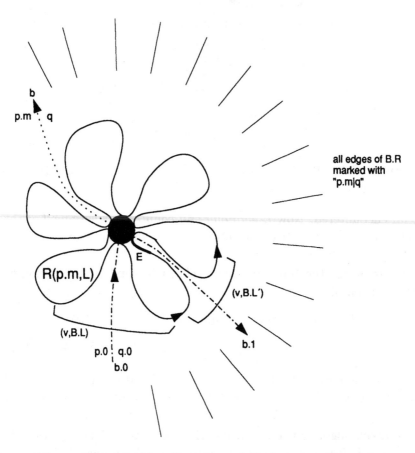

Figure 3.44: Marking the edges of B_R between E and b.

Claim 4 If $b_1.R \neq q_m$ then $b_1 = b_2$.

Proof: On the left of and close to b_1 must be a point $w \in R(p_1, L \cup R_1) \cap R(q_1, R_1)$, where $p_1 = b_1.L$ and $q_1 = b_1.R \neq q_m$, see Figure 3.45. By Lemma 3.5.2, $w \in R(q_1, R)$. Hence, $w \in R(p_1, S)$ by transitivity (Lemma 3.5.1.1). Then b_2 cannot be strictly on the left of b_1 because the area between b_0 and b_2 must be contained in R-regions of $V(S)$.   □

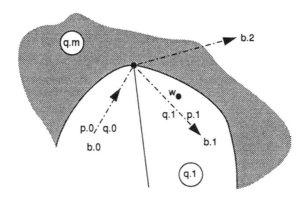

Figure 3.45: Point w belongs to $R(p_1, L \cup \text{sites}(v, B_R))$ and to $R(q_1, R)$, hence to $R(p, S)$.

Now the key observation is the following.

Claim 5 At most one piece of $R(q_m, R)$ can intersect the area on the right of the chain K containing b_0 and b_2, in a neighborhood of v.

Proof: The area on the right of K belongs to R-regions. Thus, if two petals of $R(q_m, R)$ extended to the right of K, these pieces would both belong to $R(q_m, S)$; see Figure 3.46. But since the point v belongs to $R(p_m, S)$, where $p_m < q_m$, the two pieces are disconnected—a contradiction.   □

It follows from Claims 3, 4, and 5 that b_0, b_1, and b_2 can in $R(q_m, R)$ only be situated as depicted in Figure 3.47. Note that in case e) we must have $b_1 \neq b_2$ because b_1 is a q_m-borderline w.r.t. $L \cup R_1$, but in $V(S)$ there are no points of $R(q_m, S)$ at b_1. In all other cases, $b_1 = b_2$ must hold.

If $b_1.R \neq q_m$ then $b_2 = b_1$ has already been determined (cases b), c)). Otherwise,

$$(v_R', B_R') := R\text{-endpoint}(b_1.L, q_m, (v, B_R), \text{true}, T_R)$$

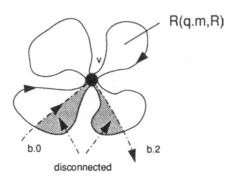

Figure 3.46: Two disconnected pieces of $R(q_m, S)$.

is invoked. If $v_R' \neq v$ then $b_1 = b_2$, and (v_R', B_R') is the endpoint of b_2 on the contour of $R(q_m, R)$ (case a)). If $v_R' = v$ then the first point of $V(R)$ induced by v in clockwise direction from (v, B_R) has been detected. We must test if b_1 is enclosed in the two outer q_m-borderlines in B_R', as in case e); if not, function R-endpoint is invoked again. Note that it is *not* necessary to *scan* the edges of B_R'. Eventually, the endpoint of $b_2 = b_1$ will be discovered (case d)), or the induced node (v, B_R') counterclockwise next to (v, B_R) is detected whose outer q_m-borderlines enclose both b_1 and b_2 (case e)).

In the latter case the situation looks as shown in Figure 3.48. At this stage, the exact location of b_2 in B_R' is still to be determined. We have depicted the case where both b_1 and b_2 are p_m-borderlines. The pointer of $\Delta(R_0)$, ρ, now points at the two outer q_m-borderlines in B_R'. Pointer λ is still situated at the endpoint of b_1 on the contour of $R(p_m, L)$. We may assume that an auxiliary pointer, λ_a, allows the last p_m-borderline encountered during the counterclockwise scan of the contour of $R(p_m, L)$ in the previous phase to be accessed. For clarity, the edges of B_R' are only indicated by dotted line segment on the circumference. Now pointer ρ is moved counterclockwise in B_R' to the position of b_1. Let $L' = \text{sites}(v, B_L')$ and $R' = \text{sites}(v, B_R')$, for short.

Claim 6 In $V(L' \cup R')$ a bisecting chain is passing through v.

Proof: The point v itself belongs to $R(p_m, S)$. Close to v are points of $R(q_m, S)$ (those on the right of the chain b_0, b_2 of $V(S)$; see Figure 3.47, e). Since $p_m \in L'$ and $q_m \in R'$ the regions of both p_m and q_m are represented at v in $V(L' \cup R')$. Thus, there must be a bisecting chain that separates them.   □

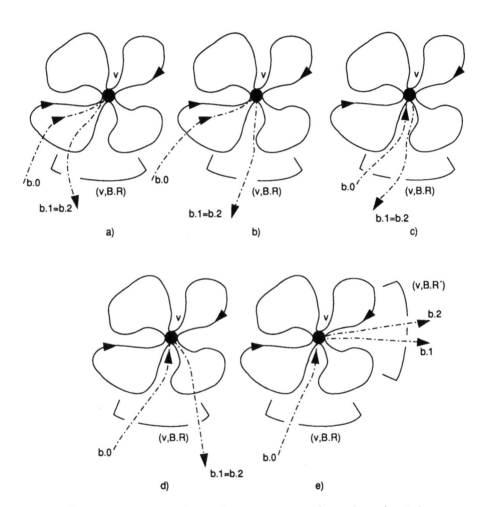

Figure 3.47: Possible configurations in $R(q_m, R)$ at (v, B_R).

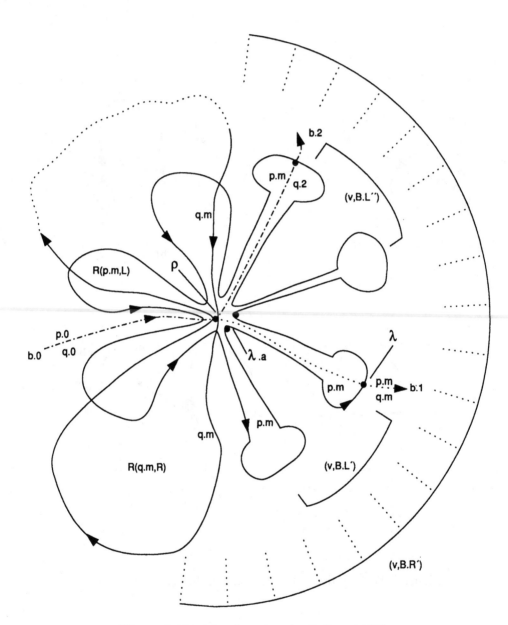

Figure 3.48: After locating (v, B_R') in $V(R)$.

Due to Claim 6,

$$b' := \text{counterclockwise-next}(b_1, (v, B_L'), (v, B_R'))$$

will not fail to report an outgoing chain segment in $V(L' \cup R')$.

Claim 7 b_2 comes before b' in counterclockwise direction from b_1.

Proof: This is certainly true if b' is a q_m-borderline; see Figure 3.49. Otherwise, b' is a borderline even in $V(L' \cup R)$. Now the proof of Claim 1 applies. □

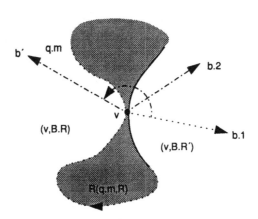

Figure 3.49: If b' is a q_m-borderline then b_2 must come first after b_1.

This enables us to run Phase 1 a second time, in order to compute b_2. Assume that b' is a $\{p', q'\}$-borderline. If $p' \neq p_m$ then b' is a borderline in $V(L \cup R')$ and must therefore be equal to b_2. Assume that $p' = p_m$. If b_1 has been a p_m-borderline, as displayed in Figure 3.48, then the next statement must be

$$(v_L', B_L') := L\text{-endpoint}(p_m, b'.R, (v', B_L'), \text{false}, T_L)$$

because this will continue the contour scan of $R(p, L)$ from the position of pointer λ. Otherwise, the value of the *entry-point* parameter in the function call must be *true*.

This time, the correct continuation, b_2, of b_0 in $V(S)$ will be detected without having to change the point induced by v in $V(R)$ again.

Of course, we have to account for the time spent on those steps in the above computation that would not have been executed in the non-degenerate case. First, we address the backtrack operations on the edges of an induced point, (v, B_R) of $V(R)$, in Phase 1. Suppose that the continuation, b, of b_0 in $V(\text{sites}(v, B_L) \cup \text{sites}(v, B_R))$ is a p_m-borderline (otherwise, $b = b_1$ and no backtracking is done); see Figure 3.44. Then only edges of B_R between b_0 and b have been marked.

Claim 8 Let c_0 be an incoming chain segment at v between b_0 and b, and assume that b is a p_m-borderline. Then the (counterclockwise first), segment c continuing c_0 in $V(\text{sites}(v, B_L') \cup \text{sites}(v, B_R))$ leaves v before b. If c, too, is a p_m-borderline then $c = b$.

Proof: Otherwise, we have the situation of Figure 3.50. Lying on the right hand side of c_0, c, the point w belongs to a region $R(q, \text{sites}(v, B_L') \cup \text{sites}(v, B_R)) \subset R(q, p_m)$, whereas, by the assumption made about b, $w \in R(p_m, \text{sites}(v, B_L) \cup \text{sites}(v, B_R)) \subset R(p_m, q)$, a contradiction. The second assertion is obvious because then c is also a borderline in $V(\text{sites}(v, B_L) \cup \text{sites}(v, B_R))$. $\square$

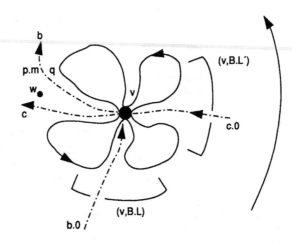

Figure 3.50: Segment c must leave v *before* b.

No matter which of the chain segments b_0, c_0 is encountered first during the merge, the computation of the second one will benefit from the marks "$p_m \mid q$" that were inscribed during the computation of the foregoing one. Figure 3.51 shows the scan history of the computation of three chain pieces, a, a_1, b_0, b_1, and c, c_1, in this order. The operations on the edges of B_R are indicated by directed lines on the circumference. Standard counterclockwise scans are denoted by solid lines, whereas dotted lines indicate backtracks during which each edge of B_R is marked with "$p_m \mid q$".

Claim 9 No edge of B_R is encountered more than three times, as vertex scans are performed on v.

Proof: Let a *successful* scan be one that leads to the correct continuing chain segment in $V(L \cup \text{sites}(v, B_R))$ (in Figure 3.51: a_1, b_1, c_1). Successful scans do not overlap since bisecting chains do not cross. During the backtrack after an unsuccessful scan, the edges of B_R are marked. No unsuccessful scan ever traverses marked edges. $\square$

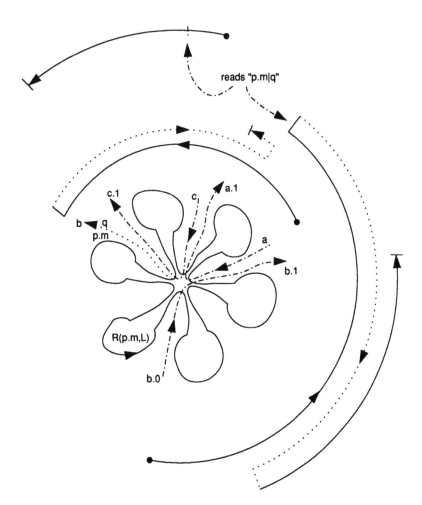

Figure 3.51: How the edges incident with an induced point (v, B_R) of $V(R)$ are scanned.

Next, we turn to the edges of $V(L)$ radiating from v. On the way from b_0 to

b_1, many induced points (v, B_L') on the contour are visited, and all the edges of B_L' scanned. This would not have been necessary if v were not a cut-point of $R(p_m, L)$, for then only the two p_m-borderlines of a vertex (v, B_L') on the contour of $R(p_m, L)$ must be checked. If (v, B_L') is a vertex of $V(L)$ (i.e., if $|B_L'| \geq 3$) no problem arises: we can charge each edge in B_L' for the extra cost, since this vertex will not be visited again by a bisecting chain, see Figure 3.8. (This argument does *not* apply to the vertices on the contour of $R(q_m, R)$ visited during the clockwise scan at the beginning of Phase 2; but the edge sets of these vertices have *not* been scanned!) There may, however, also be points (v, B_L') where B_L' consists only of the two segments of a $\{p_m, p\}$-borderline of $V(L)$ passing through v. For a fixed borderline, only one such point can be induced by v, since the region of p in $V(L)$ can be represented at v at most once, but the same borderline could run through several points, $v_1, \ldots, v_m$; see Figure 3.52. But then only one point of the $\{p_m, p\}$-borderline can be subject to the above procedure; this follows from the generalization of Theorem 3.4.1.6 to the degenerate case. Note that both (v_2, B_2) and (v_3, B_3) shown in Figure 3.52 are subject to standard contour scans performed by L-endpoint. Therefore, we may charge the cost of checking (v_1, B_1) to the $\{p_m, p\}$-edge of $V(L)$.

This shows that the merge algorithm can in fact be adapted to *degenerate* Voronoi diagrams.

Theorem 3.5.3.1 *Let $(S_0, \mathcal{J}_0)$ be an admissible curve system, and let $S_0 = L_0 \cup R_0$ be an acyclic partition. Then $\Delta(L_0)$ and $\Delta(R_0)$ can be merged into $\Delta(S_0)$ within $O(|S_0|)$ many steps using $O(|S_0|)$ storage on an $(S_0, \mathcal{J}_0)$-RAM.*

Of course, the definition of an elementary bisector operation (3.4.3.1) must also be adapted; in E3, cross-points in the sense of Definition 3.5.2.1 are addressed.

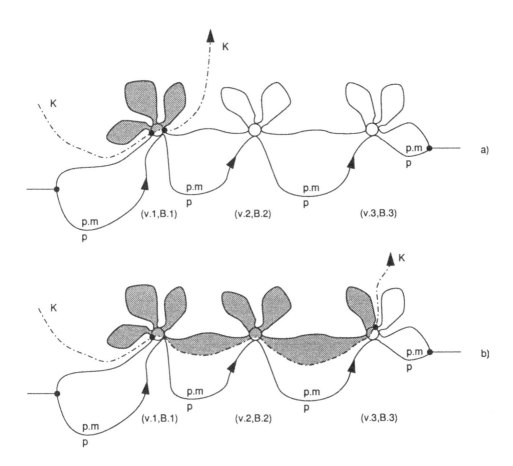

Figure 3.52: Only the point (v_1, B_1) is checked in vain during a chain continuation process. The shaded areas indicate $R(p_m, S)$.

Chapter 4

Acyclic partitions

In Chapter 1, the concept of a Voronoi diagram based on a "nice" metric in the plane has been introduced. Next, we have analyzed the structure of such diagrams under more general assumptions (Chapter 2), and shown that two diagrams $V(L_0)$ and $V(R_0)$, where $L_0 \cap R_0 = \emptyset$, can be merged within a number of steps of order $|S_0|$, $S_0 = L_0 \cup R_0$, provided that the bisector, $J(L_0', R_0')$, of arbitrary subsets $L_0' \subseteq L_0$ and $R_0' \subseteq R_0$ contains no loop (Chapter 3). Now, it remains to give sufficient criteria for the existence of such "acyclic" partitions of S_0.

The first criterion introduced in Section 4.1 generalizes the concept of supporting halfplanes from convex unit circles to the circles of a general metric. It is shown that certain classes of metrics, that satisfy this criterion, are closed under a patch operation which allows different metrics to be assigned to the regions of certain planar subdivisions.

Next, a criterion based on the simply-connectedness of the d-circles is given (Section 4.2). As an application, the metric defined by the (regular part of the) street layout of Moscow is considered (Section 4.3). It follows that the Voronoi diagram of n points in this metric can be computed in time $O(n \log n)$.

4.1 Supported d-circles

Let d be a nice metric in the plane, and assume that $S_0 = L_0 \cup R_0$ is a partition of $S_0 = S - \{\infty\}$. The first criterion to be presented is based on the following property of a metric.

Definition 4.1.1 Let α, $\overline{\alpha} \in [0, \pi)$, $\alpha \neq \overline{\alpha}$. The metric d is said to have $(\alpha, \overline{\alpha})$-*support* iff the following condition holds. Let v, w be two points on a line of slope α, let D denote the line of slope $\overline{\alpha}$ passing through w, and let H be the closed halfplane bordered by D that contains v. Then the d-circle of radius $d(v, w)$ with center in v is contained in H; see Figure 4.1.

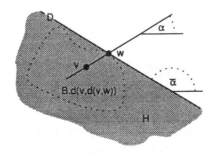

Figure 4.1: A d-circle supported by line D.

Lemma 4.1.2 *Let d be induced by a norm. Then for each $\alpha \in [0, \pi)$ there exists an $\overline{\alpha} \in [0, \pi)$ different from α such that d has $(\alpha, \overline{\alpha})$-support.*

For, a convex set admits a supporting halfplane at each boundary point.

Theorem 4.1.3 *(Klein/Wood [37]) Assume that d has $(\alpha, \overline{\alpha})$-support, and that L_0 and R_0 are separated by a line l of slope $\overline{\alpha}$. Then the partition $S_0 = L_0 \cup R_0$ is acyclic.*

Proof: Otherwise, there would exist subsets $L_0' \subseteq L_0$, $R_0' \subseteq R_0$, and a simple, bounded edge cycle, C, in $J(L_0', R_0')$ that encircles regions of one kind only, say of R_0' (cf. Remark 3.2.3). Let $q_1 \in R_0'$ be contained in the interior of C; since $S_0 \cap l = \emptyset$, the line m of slope α passing through q_1 intersects l in a point z different from q_1, see Figure 4.2. Let v be the first point of intersection of the halfline of m that radiates from q_1 and does not contain z, and C. Since C belongs to the bisector of L_0' and R_0',

$$v \in \overline{R(p, S_0')} \cap \overline{R(q, S_0')} \subset J(p, q)$$

holds, where $S_0' = L_0' \cup R_0'$, $p \in L_0'$, and $q \in R_0'$. Hence,

$$d(v, p) = d(v, q) \leq d(v, q_1),$$

because q is a nearest neigbor of v in R_0'. But p cannot belong to $B_d(v, d(v, q_1))$ since it lies on the wrong side of the line of slope $\overline{\alpha}$ through q_1—a contradiction! $\square$

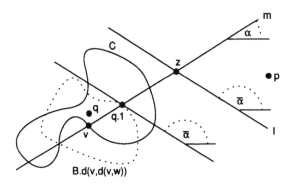

Figure 4.2: An impossible cycle.

Theorem 4.1.4 *Suppose that d is nice and has both $(\alpha, \overline{\alpha})$ and $(\beta, \overline{\beta})$-support, where $\overline{\alpha} \neq \overline{\beta}$. Let S_0 be a set of n points, and let $\mathcal{J}_0$ denote the system of bisecting curves associated with S_0. Then the Voronoi diagram $V(S_0)$ with respect to d can be computed within $O(n \log n)$ many steps and $O(n)$ storage on an $(S_0, \mathcal{J}_0)$-RAM.*

This is a consequence of Theorem 3.5.3.1 and Theorem 4.1.3, because any point set of size n can be partitioned into two subsets in such a way that the smaller one is of size at least $\lceil \frac{n-1}{4} \rceil$, by a separating line of slope $\overline{\alpha}$ or $\overline{\beta}$. Thus, recursion depth is bounded by $O(\log n)$; cf. Section 3.2.

Let $\mathcal{K}$ denote the class of all metrics d in the plane such that d induces the Euclidean topology, that all d-circles are L_2-bounded, and that for any two different points a third point metrically between them exists (properties 1),2), and 3) of Definition 1.2.12). Then d admits d-straight arcs.

Lemma 4.1.5 *Assume that $d \in \mathcal{K}$ has $(\alpha, \overline{\alpha})$-support. Then all line segments of slope α are d-straight.*

Proof: Let a, b, c be different consecutive points on a line l of slope α, as shown in Figure 4.3, a). Let $\lambda := d(a, b)$ and $\mu := d(a, c) - d(a, b)$. Since c lies above the line of slope $\overline{\alpha}$ passing through b, we have $d(a, b) < d(a, c)$. Hence $0 < \mu < d(a, c)$. We must show that $\mu = d(b, c)$ holds. When walking the line l from c to a, the distance to c changes continuously from 0 to $d(c, a)$. Thus, there exists a point $u \in \overline{ca}$ such that $d(c, u) = \mu$. The point u cannot be situated strictly between a and b on l, or the contradiction $d(a, c) \leq d(a, u) + d(u, c) < \lambda + \mu = d(a, c)$ would arise (Figure 4.3, b)).

Now let π be a d-straight arc from a to c, and let $z \in \pi$ be such that $d(c, z) = \mu$. Then, $d(a, z) = d(a, c) - \mu = \lambda$. With the orientation of Figure 4.3, a), it follows that z cannot be above the line of slope $\overline{\alpha}$ through b, nor can it be below the parallel line through u. Thus, $u = b$.   □

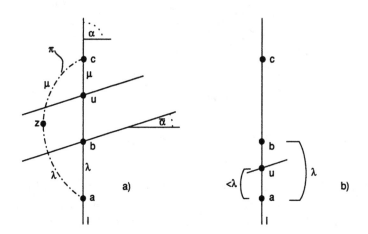

Figure 4.3: Illustrations of the proof of Lemma 4.1.5.

This lemma is a generalization of property 3) in Lemma 1.2.1.

Definition 4.1.6 Let $\mathcal{K}(\alpha, \overline{\alpha}, \beta, \overline{\beta}, \lambda, \mu)$ denote the class of all metrics d in $\mathcal{K}$ such that

1. d has both $(\alpha, \overline{\alpha})$- and $(\beta, \overline{\beta})$-support.

2. $d(a, b) = \lambda|a - b|$ if a, b are on a line of slope α.

3. $d(a, b) = \mu|a - b|$ if a, b are on a line of slope β.

Now let d_1, $d_2 \in \mathcal{K}(\alpha, \overline{\alpha}, \beta, \overline{\beta}, \lambda, \mu)$, let l denote a line of slope α, and let H_1, H_2 denote the closed halfplanes separated by l. Then a new metric d, called a *composition of d_1 and d_2 along l*, can be defined as follows. Let π be an arc in the plane that crosses l at most finitely often and is of finite length in both d_1 and d_2; see Figure 4.4. Then π consists of finitely many segments, σ, each of which is entirely contained in H_1, in H_2, or in both. In the first case, we put $\lambda(\sigma) := \lambda_{d_1}(\sigma)$, in the second case $\lambda(\sigma) := \lambda_{d_2}(\sigma)$. If $\sigma \subset H_1 \cap H_2 = l$ then its d_1-length equals the d_2-length. Let $\lambda(\pi)$ denote the sum over all $\lambda(\sigma)$, where $\sigma \subset \pi$.

Now let

$$d(a, c) := \inf_\pi \lambda(\pi),$$

the infimum taken over all arcs π as above that join a with c. We observe that the infimum is actually a minimum: if σ is a segment of π with endpoints v, w on

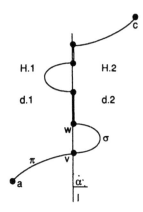

Figure 4.4: Defining the composition of two metrics.

l then $\lambda(\pi)$ can only become smaller if σ is replaced with the line segment $\overline{vw}$, the latter being d_1- and d_2-straight according to Lemma 4.1.5. Thus, if $a \in H_1$ and $c \in H_2$ then only such arcs need to be considered that cross line l once, and consist of straight segments only. Hence, $d(a, c) = \inf_{b\in l}(d_1(a, b) + d_2(b, c))$. If $|b_n| \longrightarrow \infty$ then $d_1(a, b_n) \longrightarrow \infty$, because the d_1-circles are bounded w.r.t. $|\cdot|$. Therefore, the infimum is taken in a compact segment of l. Here it becomes a minimum, by continuity. One obtains

$$
*) \qquad d(a, c) = \begin{cases} d_1(a, c) & \text{if } a, c \in H_1. \\ d_2(a, c) & \text{if } a, c \in H_2. \\ \min_{b\in l}(d_1(a, b) + d_2(b, c)) & \text{if } a \in H_1, b \in H_2. \end{cases}
$$

It follows (either by a direct proof, or from the criterion given in §16, [53]) that d is a metric in $\mathcal{K}$.

Claim $d \in \mathcal{K}(\alpha, \overline{\alpha}, \beta, \overline{\beta}, \lambda, \mu)$.

Proof: Clearly, property 2) is fulfilled since the line l is of slope α. Next, we demonstrate that d has $(\alpha, \overline{\alpha})$-support. To this end, let v and w be two points on a line of slope α in H_1, and assume that $d(v, q) \leq d(v, w)$ holds for a point q. We must show that q and v lie on the same side of the line D of slope $\overline{\alpha}$ through w. This is immediate if $q \in H_1$ (due to $*$), and because d_1 has $(\alpha, \overline{\alpha})$-support. Assume that $q \in H_2$ and that q and v are separated by D. Let $\{z\} = \pi \cap l$, where π is a d-straight arc from v to q; see Figure 4.5.

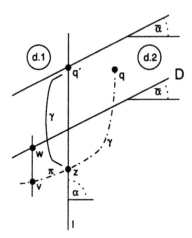

Figure 4.5: $d(v, q) \leq d(v, w)$ is impossible in this situation.

We choose a point q' on l above z such that $d_2(z, q') = d_2(z, q)$ holds. Since d_2 has $(\alpha, \overline{\alpha})$-support, q lies on or below the line of slope $\overline{\alpha}$ through q', and above the line D, by assumption. Hence, q' lies above D, and we obtain the contradiction

$$
\begin{aligned}
d_1(v, q') &\leq d_1(v, z) + d_2(z, q') \\
&= d_1(v, z) + d_2(z, q) \\
&= d(v, q) \leq d(v, w) = d_1(v, w).
\end{aligned}
$$

Next, we prove that d fulfills property 3) of Definition 4.1.6. Let a, c be points on a line of slope β. If $\overline{ac} \subset H_1$, or $\overline{ac} \subset H_2$, then the assertion is obvious. Assume that $a \in H_1$, $c \in H_2$, and let $\{b\} = \overline{ac} \cap l$. Clearly,

$$
d(a, c) \leq d_1(a, b) + d_2(b, c) = \mu |a - b| + \mu |b - c| = \mu |a - c|.
$$

Suppose that $d(a, c)$ is less than the right hand side. Let π be a d-straight arc from a to c, and let $\{b'\} = \pi \cap l$. Then

$$
d(a, c) = d_1(a, b') + d_2(b', c) < d_1(a, b) + d_2(b, c).
$$

W.l.o.g. assume that $d_1(a, b') < d_1(a, b)$. Let $w \in \overline{ab}$ be such that $d_1(a, w) = d_1(a, b')$, see Figure 4.6. Then $w \neq b$, and a and b' lie on the same side of the line of slope $\overline{\beta}$, W, through w (d_1 has $(\beta, \overline{\beta})$-support). This implies $d_2(c, b) < d_2(c, b')$ because c and b' are separated by the line B of slope $\overline{\beta}$ passing through b (d_2 has $(\beta, \overline{\beta})$-support). Let $z \in \pi \mid_{[b', c]}$ be such that $d_2(c, z) = d_2(c, b)$. Then c and z are not separated by B. Finally, let B' denote the line of slope β through b', and let $\{r\} = B' \cap B$. From d_2 having properties 1) and 3) it follows that $d_2(w, b) \leq d_2(b', r) \leq d_2(b', z)$, which, by $d_1(w, b) = d_2(w, b)$, yields the contradiction

$$
\begin{aligned}
d_1(a, b) + d_2(b, c) &= d_1(a, w) + d_1(w, b) + d_2(b, c) \\
&\leq d_1(a, b') + d_2(b', z) + d_2(z, c) \\
&= d(a, c).
\end{aligned}
$$

It remains to show that d has $(\beta, \bar{\beta})$-support. So, let v, w be on a line of slope β, and assume that the line of slope $\bar{\beta}$, W, through w separates v from a point q that fulfills $d(v, q) \leq d(v, w)$. If v, w, q are contained in the same halfplane H_i then the contradiction is immediate. Let $v, q \in H_1$ and $w \in H_2$ (Figure 4.7). Then one obtains

$$
d_1(v, q) = d(v, q) \leq d(v, w) = \mu|v - w| = d_1(v, w)
$$

by what was shown just before, a contradiction. Assume that $v \in H_1$ and w, $q \in H_2$, as shown in Figure 4.8. Let π a d-straight arc from v to q, and let $\{z\} = \pi \cap l$.

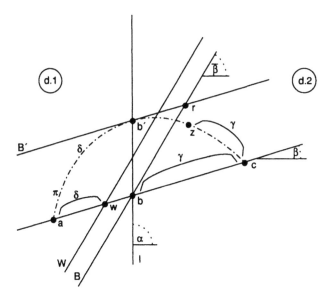

Figure 4.6: Segments of slope $\bar{\beta}$ are straight in d.

Let Z denote the line of slope β through z, and let $q' \in H_2 \cap Z$ be such that $d_2(z, q) = d_2(z, q')$. Then z, q are not separated by the line of slope $\bar{\beta}$ passing through q'. Similary, let $v' \in H_1 \cap Z$ such that $d_1(z, v) = d_1(z, v')$. Then

$$
\mu|v' - q'| = d(v', q')
$$

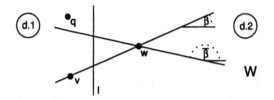

Figure 4.7: Here, $d(v, q) \le d(v, w)$ is impossible.

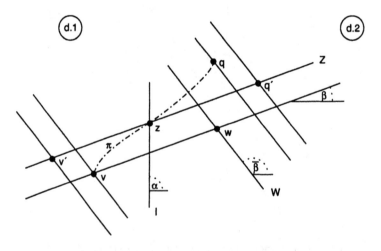

Figure 4.8: Here, $d(v, q) \le d(v, w)$ is impossible, too.

$$
\begin{aligned}
&= d_1(v', z) + d_2(z, q') \\
&= d_1(v, z) + d_2(z, q) \\
&= d(v, q) \\
&\leq d(v, w) \\
&= \mu|v - w|,
\end{aligned}
$$

a contradiction, because at least the lines of slope $\overline{\beta}$ through w and q are different. The remaining case $(v, w \in H_1, q \in H_2)$ is simpler. $\qquad\qquad\square$

Thus, we have shown the following theorem.

Theorem 4.1.7 *The class* $\mathcal{K}(\alpha, \overline{\alpha}, \beta, \overline{\beta}, \lambda, \mu)$ *is closed under composition of metrics along lines of slope* α *or* β.

Let P be a fixed parallelogram with center 0, and let v and w denote two points on adjacent edges of P. Furthermore, let $F(P)$ denote the family of all norms whose unit circle fits into P, when centered at 0, and touches v and w, see Figure 4.9. Finally, let α, β denote the angles of v and w, and let $\overline{\alpha}, \overline{\beta}$ the angles of the corresponding edges of P.

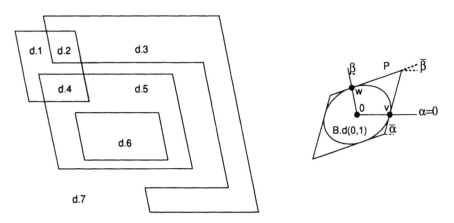

Figure 4.9: A composition of metrics.

Corollary 4.1.8 Let X be a (v, w)-oriented partition of the plane. Assume that d is the composite metric obtained by assigning an arbitrary element of $F(P)$ to each region in X. Then $d \in \mathcal{K}(\alpha, \overline{\alpha}, \beta, \overline{\beta}, |v|^{-1}, |w|^{-1})$.

After refining X to a complete (v, w)-grid, this can be proven by induction on the number of separating lines, using the theorem. Theorem 4.1.4 applies to a metric out of such a class if the bisectors $J(p, q)$ fulfill the (technical) condition 4) of the definition of a nice metric.

Though supported metrics bear a resemblance to norms, they are different in some aspects. In the composite metric d depicted in Figure 4.10, for example, either of the two arcs from a to c is d-straight, but none of them can be continued. This would not happen with the L_2-norm inside the rectangle, and the L_1-norm outside.

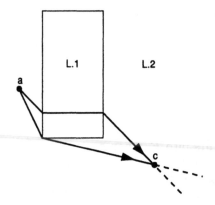

Figure 4.10: None of the d-straight arcs can be continued beyond c.

4.2   Simply-connected d-circles

In this section, one more tool from the theory of metric spaces will be needed.

Lemma 4.2.1 *Let d be nice, and assume that $a_n \longrightarrow a$, $b_n \longrightarrow b$ hold for sequences (a_n), (b_n) of points. Let π_n be a d-straight arc from a_n to b_n. Then there exist a d-straight arc π from a to b, and a sequence (n_k) such that $\pi_{n_k} \longrightarrow \pi$ holds in the following sense. For suitable parametrizations f_{n_k} of π_{n_k} and f of π we have*

$$\sup_{t \in [0,1]} |f(t) - f_{n_k}(t)| \leq \epsilon$$

for all k sufficiently large.

This implies that almost all π_{n_k} are contained in the stripe of (Euclidean) breadth 2ϵ around π.

Proof: If $d(a, a_n) \leq \eta$ and $d(b, b_n) \leq \eta$ then (cf. proof of Lemma 1.2.2) $d(a_n, b_n) \leq d(a, b) + 2\eta$. Thus, for each $z \in \pi_n$

$$d(a, z) \leq d(a, a_n) + d(a_n, z) \leq d(a, a_n) + d(a_n, b_n) \leq d(a, b) + 3\eta =: r,$$

showing that (almost) all d-straight arcs are contained in the compact set $B_d(a, r)$. Now the assertion follows from 13., §17, [53] in combination with 7., §17, and 3., §11, and with 9. and 13., §9, loc. cit. □

Now we show that the Voronoi regions in a nice metric do not look as ugly as general abstract Voronoi regions can (cf. Figure 3.30 and Theorem 2.5.5).

Lemma 4.2.2 *Let d be a nice metric. Then each Voronoi region with respect to d has a connected interior.*

Proof: According to Theorem 1.2.13 each Voronoi region $R(p, S)$ is connected, no matter which order $<$ on the set of sites is chosen in Definition 1.2.3. If there were a cut point in $R(p, S)$ separating points of the interior then changing $<$ such that p becomes the maximum in S would cause $R(p, S)$ to become disconnected, due to Theorem 2.3.5. □

The next criterion for a partition of S_0 to be acyclic is based on the following property of a metric. A set $A \subseteq \Re^2$ is called *simply-connected* iff for each simple closed curve $C \subset A$ the inner domain, $I(C)$, of C is also contained in A (intuitively, iff A has no holes).

Theorem 4.2.3 *Let d be a nice metric all of whose circles are simply-connected. Let l be a bisecting curve separating L_0 from R_0, such that for each d-circle the intersection $B_d(c, r) \cap l$ is connected (possibly empty). Then $S_0 = L_0 \cup R_0$ is an acyclic partition.*

Proof: As in the proof of Theorem 4.1.3, we assume that there exist $L'_0 \subseteq L_0$, $R'_0 \subseteq R_0$, and a simple, bounded edge cycle C in $J(L'_0, R'_0)$ such that precisely the regions $R(q_i, S'_0)$, $i = 1, \ldots, m$, are encircled by C, where $q_i \in R'_0$ for $i = 1, \ldots, m$ and $S'_0 = L'_0 \cup R'_0$. As a curve, C need not be simple; some pieces of C may be squeezed together. Then its interior consists of finitely many domains. Let D be one of them. According to Lemma 4.2.2, if $w \in D \cap R(q_i, S'_0)$ then $q_i \in D$. Thus, for $R''_0 := R'_0 \cap D$ we obtain the following.

Claim 1 $z \in \partial D \implies \exists p \in L'_0, q \in R''_0 : z \in \overline{R(p, S'_0)} \cap \overline{R(q, S'_0)}$

Hence, any $z \in \partial D$ is the limit of a sequence of elements $z_n \in R(p, S'_0)$, where $p \in L'_0$. For each z_n, there exists a d-straight arc π_n from p to z_n. Since the region of p is d-star-shaped, we have $\pi_n \subset R(p, S'_0)$, hence $\pi_n \cap D = \emptyset$ (each point in D belongs to a region of a point in R''_0). An application of Lemma 4.2.1 yields

Claim 2   For each $z \in \partial D$ there exists a d-straight arc, π_z, to a nearest neighbor of z in L'_0, such that $\pi_z \cap D = \emptyset$.

For convenience, assume that the bisecting curve l is oriented in such a way that the points of L_0 are on the left. Let H_L, H_R denote the domains on the left and on the right of l.

Case 1: $\partial D \cap l \neq \emptyset$. Let α and ω denote the first and the last point of l contained in ∂D, correspondingly. Let A denote the part of ∂D between α and ω that becomes accessible from H_R if $l \mid [\alpha, \omega]$ is removed; see Figure 4.11. Clearly, *if $z \in A$ then an arc π_z, as of Claim 2, cannot run to a point in L'_0 without intersecting l below α or above ω. Let z' denote the first point on π_z of this kind, as seen from z.*

Claim 3   Let $h \in \pi_y \mid [y, y'] \cap \pi_z \mid [z, z']$, where $y, z \in A$. Then the concatenation of $\pi_y \mid [y, h]$ and $\pi_z \mid [h, p_z]$ is d-straight, and the endpoint of π_z, p_z, is a nearest neighbor of y in L'_0; see Figure 4.12.

Proof: Since p_z is a nearest neighbor of z in L'_0, we have

$$d(z, h) + d(h, p_z) = d(z, p_z) \leq d(z, p_y) \leq d(z, h) + d(h, p_y)$$

which implies $d(h, p_z) \leq d(h, p_y)$. Since p_y is a nearest neighbor of y, one obtains

$$\lambda_d(\pi_y \mid [y, h]) + \lambda_d(\pi_z \mid [h, p_z]) = d(y, h) + d(h, p_z) \leq d(y, h) + d(h, p_y)$$
$$= d(y, p_y) \leq d(y, p_z),$$

and both assertions follow (in fact, equality holds everywhere). $\square$

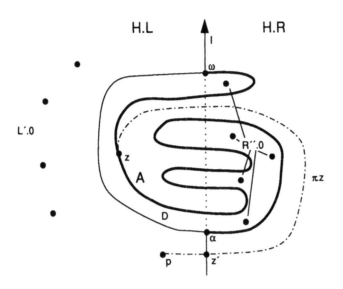

Figure 4.11: With $l \mid [\alpha, \omega]$ removed, A is accessible from H_R.

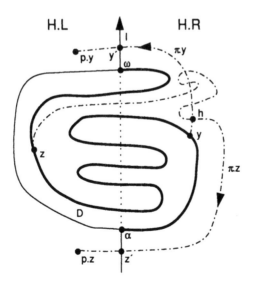

Figure 4.12: $\pi_y \mid [y, h] \circ \pi_z \mid [h, p_z]$ is also d-straight.

Now the discussion of Case 1 is continued.

Case 1.1   For each $z \in A$, the point z' is below α.
Let

2) $$w \in \overline{R(p', S_0')} \cap \overline{R(q, S_0')} \subset J(p', q),$$

according to 1). Then the d-circle $B = B_d(w, d(w, w'))$ contains w and w' (see
Figure 4.13). Thus, B also contains $l \mid [w', w]$. By assumption, $\pi_w \mid [w, w']$ is
contained in B. Together, these two segments form a simple closed curve in B
that encircles $R_0'' \ni q$. But the point q is *not* contained in B, due to

$$d(w, q) = d(w, p') \geq d(w, p_w) > d(w, w')$$

(the equality follows from 2); p_w is a nearest neighbor of w in L_0', due to Claim
2, and not contained in l). Then the d-circle B cannot be simply-connected, a
contradiction.

The proof is symmetric if all points z' are above w.

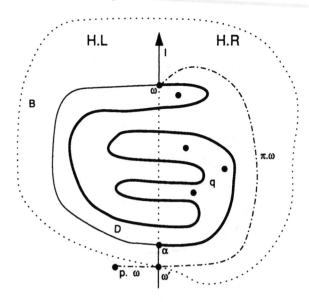

Figure 4.13: Illustration of Case 1.1.

Case 1.2 There exist y, z in A such that y' is above w and z' is below α.
The key is in proving the following.

Claim 4: There exists a point c in A and *two d-straight paths*, π_1 and π_2, leading from c to nearest neighbors p_1, p_2 of c in L'_0, such that c'_1 is above ω and c'_2 is below α and that $\pi_1 \mid [c, c'_1]$, $\pi_2 \mid [c, c'_2]$ do not cross.

A similar assertion was first used in [14] for convex distance functions. In that case, the existence of c and π_1, π_2 is quite obvious because straight line segments are d-straight, so that a rightmost point c of A will do (consider straight line segments leading to points that lie slightly above and below c). Here, we proceed as follows.

Proof: Let y, z be as in the statement of Case 1.2. If $\pi_y \mid [y, y']$ and $\pi_z \mid [z, z']$ cross, let h denote the last point on π_z that belongs to the intersection of both (cf. Figure 4.12). By Claim 3, $\pi_1 := \pi_y$ and $\pi_2 := \pi_y \mid [y, h] \circ \pi_z \mid [h, p_z]$ have the required properties, after splicing $\pi_y \mid [y, h]$.
Now assume that p_y and p_z do not cross between y, y', and z, z', correspondingly. Should y equal z we put $\pi_1 := \pi_y, \pi_2 := \pi_z$. Otherwise, we define

$$y_1 := y, \quad \rho_1 := \pi_y,$$
$$z_1 := z, \quad \sigma_1 := \pi_z.$$

Let $f(t)$ be a parametrization of A, and assume that $y_1 = f(r_1)$ and $z_1 = f(s_1)$, where $0 \leq r_1 < s_1 \leq 1$. Now let

$$t := \frac{s_1 + r_1}{2} \qquad \text{and} \qquad v := f(t).$$

Then v lies between y_1 and z_1 on A, as depicted in Figure 4.14. We may assume that $\pi_v \mid [v, v']$ does not cross $\sigma_1 \mid [y_1, y'_1]$ or $\rho_1 \mid [z_1, z'_1]$ (otherwise, we would replace the segment of π_v after the first point of intersection, using Claim 3 again). The point v' is either above ω or below α. Assume that the latter case applies. Then we put

$$y_2 := y_1, \quad \rho_2 := \rho_1, \quad r_2 := r_1$$
$$z_2 := v, \quad \sigma_2 := \pi_v, \quad s_2 := t$$

and iterate the procedure. By construction, the sequences (r_m) and (t_m) tend to a common limit, λ. Therefore, if $c := f(\lambda)$ then $y_n \longrightarrow c \longleftarrow z_n$ holds on A. Since L'_0 is a finite set, there exists an infinite subsequence (ρ_{n_k}) of (ρ_n) all of whose members have the same endpoint, p_1, in L'_0. By Lemma 4.2.1, a subsequence of (ρ_{n_k}) converges to a d-straight arc, π_1, from c to p_1. π_1 must have its point c_1 above ω because this holds for all ρ_{n_k}. The arc π_2 is constructed in the same way, see Figure 4.15. The arcs π_1 and π_2 do not cross. $\square$

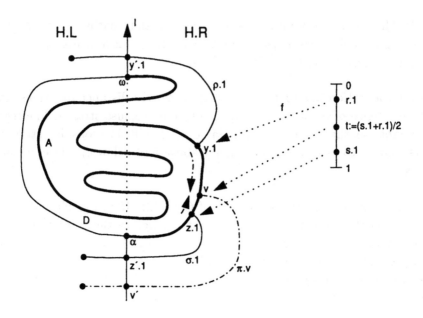

Figure 4.14: Construction of arcs.

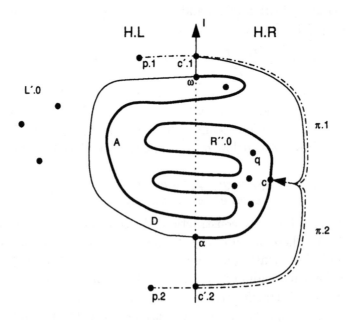

Figure 4.15: Construction of π_1 and π_2.

Now Case 1.2 can be settled in the same way as Case 1.1. Assume that $d(c, c_1') \le d(c, c_2')$, and let

$$B := B_d(c, d(c, c_2')).$$

Then the closed curve $l \mid [c_2', c_1'] \circ \pi_1 \mid [c_1', c] \circ \pi_2 \mid [c, c_2']$ belongs to B. It includes a simple closed curve encircling R_0'', which leads to the same contradiction as before.

The Case 2, where $\partial D \cap l = \emptyset$, is analogous to Case 1.2. Thereby, the proof of Theorem 4.2.3 is completed. $\qquad\qquad\qquad\qquad\qquad\qquad\qquad\qquad\qquad\qquad \Box$

In Section 4.3 an application of this theorem is discussed.

4.3 The Moscow metric

Most of the streets of Moscow are either radii emanating from the Kremlin, or pieces of circles around it. This pattern can also be found in the maps of other cities like Karlsruhe, for example; see Figure 4.16 as of [20].

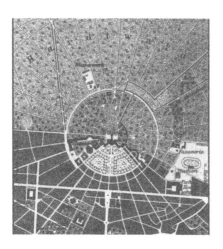 

Figure 4.16: The maps of Karlsruhe and Moscow.

To give a precise definition, let 0 denote the origin in the plane. In the following, 0 will also be referred to as the *center*.

Definition 4.3.1 Let A be the set of all arcs that consist of finitely many segments of radii from 0 and circles around 0. Let $A_{a,b}$ denote the arcs of A that join a with b.

Then

$$d_M(a,b) := \inf_{\alpha \in A_{a,b}} \lambda_{L_2}(\alpha)$$

is called the *Moscow-distance* of a and b. As usual, L_2 denotes the Euclidean norm.

Each arc α in A has a finite Euclidean length. The function d_M is a metric that induces the Euclidean topology. Its circles are bounded in L_2. These properties can easily be verified directly.

We are using the following notations. Let $\alpha \in A_{a,b}$. The *type* of a circular segment of α is C^+, if it is counterclockwise oriented, and C^-, otherwise. A radial segment is of type R^+, if it runs away from the center, and of type R^-, otherwise. By combining successive segments of the same type into one, the decomposition of α into *maximal* segments is obtained. The *type of* α is the word that consists of the consecutive types of the maximal segments of α (Figure 4.17, 1)). It cannot contain the subwords C^+C^-, C^-C^+, R^+R^-, because α is simple, and R^-R^+ can only occur if R^- ends at the center. The *size* of α is the number of maximal segments. An arc of size ≤ 2 in $A_{a,b}$ is uniquely determined by its type.

In order to determine the d_M-straight arcs we first prove the following.

Lemma 4.3.2 *Let $\alpha \in A_{a,b}$ be of size 3. Then there exists an arc $\beta \in A_{a,b}$ of size ≤ 2 that is shorter (in L_2) than α, unless α is of type R^-CR^+ where the angle of C included by R^- and R^+ equals 2, in radiant measure. In this case, all such arcs of type R^-CR^+ and R^-R^+ in $A_{a,b}$ are of the same length.*

Proof: By case analysis, using the following facts. Let C be one of C^-, C^+. If an arc is of type CR^-R^+ or R^-R^+C then the arc R^-R^+ is shorter (Figure 4.17, 2)). The arc CR^+ is shorter than R^+C; symmetrically, R^-C is shorter than CR^- (Figure 4.17, 3)). Finally, let α be of type R^-CR^+, as depicted in Figure 4.18. Let ϕ denote the angle between the two radii, as covered by the C segment. Assume w.l.o.g. that a and b have the same distance r_2 from the center, and suppose that the endpoints of C have distance r_1. Let β and γ be as in Figure 4.18. Then

$$\lambda_{L_2}(\alpha) = 2(r_2 - r_1) + \phi r_1$$
$$\lambda_{L_2}(\beta) = \phi r_2$$
$$\lambda_{L_2}(\gamma) = 2r_2$$

which shows that β is shorter than α iff $\phi < 2$, and γ is shorter than α iff $\phi > 2$. If $\phi = 2$ then β, γ, and all arcs α that arise when r_1 ranges over $(0, r_2)$ have the

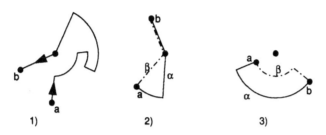

Figure 4.17: 1) An arc of type $R^-C^+R^+C^-R^+C^+R^-R^+$. 2) and 3) Arc β is shorter than α.

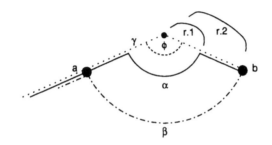

Figure 4.18: Which of α, β, γ is shortest depends on the angle ϕ.

same length. $\square$

Now let $\alpha \in A_{a,b}$. As long as size$(\alpha) \geq 4$ we can find a shorter arc in $A_{a,b}$ of smaller size, by applying Lemma 4.3.2 to a subarc of size 3 whose type is different from R^-CR^+. The discussion in the above proof shows that the minimum length arcs of size ≤ 3 in $A_{a,b}$ are precisely those depicted in Figure 4.19 (the case where one of a, b coincides with the center can be considered a special case of 1) or 2)). It follows that the infimum in the definition of d_M is a minimum, achieved by exactly the arcs of Figure 4.19.

Lemma 4.3.3   *1. Exactly the arcs depicted in Figure 4.19 are d_M-straigth.*

2. The d_M-circles are simply-connected.

Proof: 1)   The d_M-length of an element of $A_{a,b}$ can never exceed its L_2-length (which has been used for defining d_M). Since the arcs shown in Figure 4.19 have an L_2-length equal to $d_M(a,b)$, this must be their d_M-length, too. Hence, these arcs are d_M-straight. In particular, any two points can be joined by a d_M-straight arc. It remains to show that no further d_M-straight arcs exist. Assume

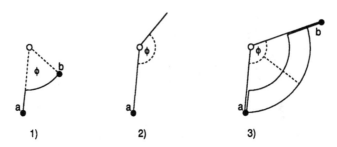

Figure 4.19: Minimum length arcs. 1) $\phi < 2$. 2) $\phi > 2$. 3) $\phi = 2$.

that $d_M(a,b) + d_M(b,c) = d_M(a,c)$ holds, and let α, β be arcs of minimum L_2-length, that join a with b and b with c. Then $\alpha \circ \beta$ is again of minimum L_2-length (cf. the proof of Corollary 1.2.11). Consequently, each point b on a d_M-straight arc π between a and c must lie on an L_2-minimal arc.

In case 1) and 2) of Figure 4.19, only one such arc exists which must be equal to π. If a and c include an angle of 2 (case 3)) we choose a point v on π, different from the center, such that none of the angles $\angle(a,v)$ and $\angle(v,c)$ equals 2, and apply the same argument to the resulting subarcs of π.

2)   An inspection of Figure 4.19 shows that each d_M-straight arc can be continued to infinity at either end. Assume that the simple closed curve K is contained in a d_M-circle $B_{d_M}(p,r)$, and let $z \in I(K)$. Let α be a d_M-straight arc from p to z; the continuation, A, of α must hit K somewhere, say at point v (Figure 4.20). Since $A \mid [p,v]$ is d_M-straight, we obtain $d_M(p,z) < d_M(p,v) \leq r$; thus, z belongs to $B_{d_M}(p,r)$.   □

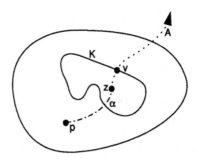

Figure 4.20: A metric whose straight arcs can be continued has simply-connected circles $B_d(p,r)$.

The next lemma shows that the conditions of Theorem 4.2.3 can be fulfilled if lines through the center are used as separating curves.

Lemma 4.3.4 *The intersection of a straight line through the center and a d_M-circle is connected.*

Proof: Let l be a line passing through 0, and let l_1, l_2 denote the halflines radiating from 0. Assume that v, w belong to $l \cap B_{d_M}(p, r)$. We must show that $l \mid_{[v,w]}$ is contained in $B := B_{d_M}(p, r)$, too.

Suppose that $v \in l_1$ and $w \in l_2$. Then the center must be contained in B. For, if none of v, w, p equals 0 then at least one of the angles $\angle(v, p), \angle(w, p)$ must be greater than 1. If $\angle(v, p) = \phi > 1$ then a d_M-straight arc, α, from p to v either runs through the center (if $\phi \geq 2$), or is longer than the straight arc $\overline{p0}$; see Figure 4.21, 1). Thus, we may assume that both v and w belong to l_1.

Suppose that $|v| > |w|$, and let $\phi = \angle(v, p)$. If $\phi = 0$ or $\phi \geq 2$ or $|p| \leq |w|$ then the assertion follows. Otherwise, the d_M-straight arc to w is of type $R^- C$, the arc to v of type $R^- C, C$, or CR^+, as shown in Figure 4.21, 2). With the notations of the figure, we have

$$
\begin{aligned}
d_M(p, v) &\geq d_M(p, v') = \phi r_2 \\
d_M(p, z) &= \phi r + r_2 - r \\
d_M(p, w) &= \phi r_1 + r_2 - r_1
\end{aligned}
$$

which shows that $d_M(p, z) \leq d_M(p, v)$ if $\phi \geq 1$, and $d_M(p, z) \leq d_M(p, w)$ if $\phi \leq 1$. Thus, $z \in B$. □

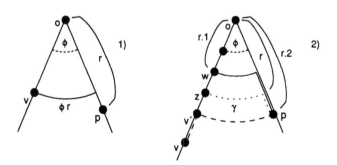

Figure 4.21: 1) If $\phi > 1$ then 0 is closer to p than v. 2) Arc γ cannot exceed in length both the arc to v' and the arc to w.

Figure 4.22 displays a system of d_M-circles expanding from a point c.

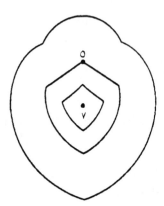

Figure 4.22: d_M-circles expanding from v.

A technical task still remains: the determination of the bisectors in d_M. Let $q = (s, 0)$ be a point different from 0, in polar coordinates; here the first component gives the (positive) L_2-distance of q from 0, whereas the second entry denotes its angle in $[0, 2\pi)$ with respect to the negative y-axis. According to Lemma 4.3.3, the shape of a d_M-straight arc from q to a point z depends on the location of z. Figure 4.23 depicts the six areas of "equal arc shape"; for all points $z = (t, \alpha)$ of the same area, A_q, $d_M(q, z)$ can be expressed by a closed formula, $F_{A_q}(t, \alpha)$.

Now let $p = (r, \phi)$ be a second point, and assume $r < s$. In order to compute the bisector $B(p, q)$, the maps induced by q and p must be superimposed. Three cases arise, depending on the size of ϕ (Figure 4.24).

For each of the resulting 18 sub-areas, $A_q \cap A_p$, the part of $B(p, q)$ contained herein is the (possibly empty) set of all points (t, α) satisfying

$$(t, \alpha) \in A_q \cap A_p \quad \& \quad F_{A_q}(t, \alpha) = F_{A_p}(t, \alpha).$$

This leads to three types of equations

$$\alpha = \alpha_0$$
$$t = t_0$$
$$(\alpha - \alpha_0)(t - t_0) = c \neq 0$$

showing that *in polar coordinates*, $B(p, q)$ is a curve consisting of a bounded number of "line" segments and "hyperbola" segments. In Cartesian coordinates, the first equation describes a line through 0, the second a circle with center in 0, and the third a curve whose equation involves trigonometric functions.

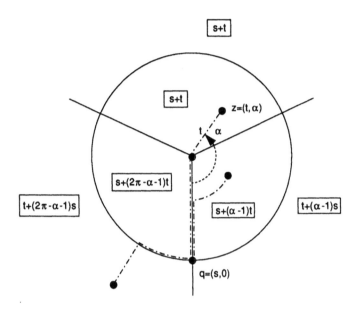

Figure 4.23: The areas of equal straight arc shape induced by point q, and the associated formulae.

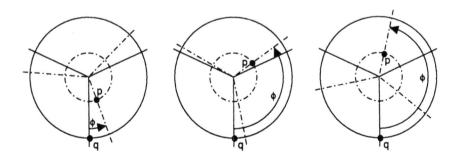

Figure 4.24: 1) $0 \leq \phi \leq 2$. 2) $2 \leq \phi \leq 2\pi - 4$. 3) $2\pi - 4 \leq \phi < 2\pi$.

Not each of the 18 sub-areas of the superimposed maps can contain a piece of $B(p,q)$. It turns out that $B(p,q)$ consists of at most 8 segments; this can only happen in case 3) of Figure 4.24. Figure 4.25 gives an example, here $\phi = \pi$, $r = 2$, and $s = 3$.

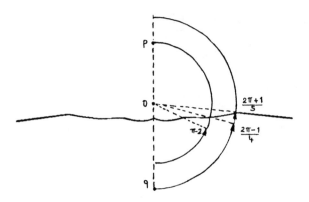

Figure 4.25: A bisector consisting of 8 segments. 1) $x = \frac{1}{2-\alpha}$ for $\alpha \in [0, \pi - 2]$. 2) $x = \frac{1}{\pi - 2\alpha}$ for $\alpha \in [\pi - 2, \frac{2\pi-1}{4}]$. 3) $x = \frac{9-2\pi}{2-\alpha}$ for $\alpha \in [\frac{2\pi-1}{4}, \frac{2\pi+1}{5}]$. 4) $\alpha = \frac{2\pi+1}{5}$.

In Figure 4.26 a bisecting curve consisting of 6 segments is shown that contains a piece of a circle. Here, $\phi = \frac{3}{2}$, $r = 2$, and $s = 3$. The curve equations in left-to-right order are: $\alpha = 2\pi - \frac{5}{3}$, $x = \frac{1}{2+\alpha-2\pi}$, $x = \frac{2}{3}$, $x = \frac{1}{\frac{3}{2}-2\alpha}$, $x = \frac{6}{2-\alpha} - 2$, $\alpha = \frac{4}{5}$.

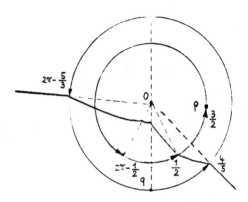

Figure 4.26: A d_M-bisector containing a circular segment.

It is clear that only a radial curve segment can be unbounded: if $z \in B(p,q)$

and $\mid z \mid > s$ then each d-straight arc from z to p or to q must begin with a radial segment R^- that leads at least as far as to the circle containing q. The piece of R^- between z and this circle belongs to $B(p,q)$, too.

A special situation occurs if p and q have the same Euclidean distance to the center, i.e., if $s = r$, provided that the two areas A_q and A_p, that are accessed via the center, overlap (case 1) and 2) in Figure 4.24). Here the defining equation for $B(p,q) \cap A_q \cap A_p$ reads as $x + r = x + s$, which is void since $r = s$. Thus, the whole area of $A_q \cap A_p$ belongs to $B(p,q)$, see Figure 4.27. If we fix the lexicographic order in the plane for breaking bisector ties (cf. Definition 1.2.3) then, in the situation of Figure 4.27, the clockwise most boundary of $B(p,q)$ will be chosen as $J(p,q)$. Summarizing, we have seen that the Moscow metric, d_M, is nice.

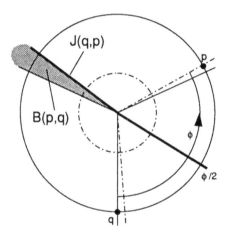

Figure 4.27: A d_M-bisector that contains a region.

Theorem 4.3.5 *The d_M-Voronoi diagram of n points in the plane can be computed in optimal time $O(n \log n)$ and space $O(n)$ on a real RAM.*

Proof: First, we compute the polar coordinates of the given points, and sort them on their polar angles as the major key, and on their L_2-distance from the center as the minor key. Then, we run the divide-and-conquer algorithm, using a straight line passing through the center, in order to split the point set into subsets, L_0 and R_0, such that the numbers of different polar angles occuring in L_0 and R_0 are equal, up to one. Due to the Lemmata 4.3.3, 4.3.4, and Theorem 4.2.3, the resulting partition is acyclic. The d_M-Voronoi diagram of m points on the same ray emanating from the center can be computed in time $O(m)$, if the points are sorted; see Figure 4.28. According to the results of Chapter 3, the subdiagrams can be merged in a number of steps proportional to $|L_0 \cup R_0|$. Since the elementary bisector operations (Definition 3.4.3.1) can be carried out in constant time each (on a real RAM), the result follows.   □

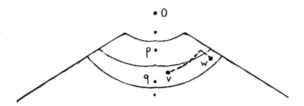

Figure 4.28: The d_M-Voronoi diagram of points of the same polar angle.

Figure 4.29 shows the d_M-Voronoi diagram of a set of irregularly placed points.

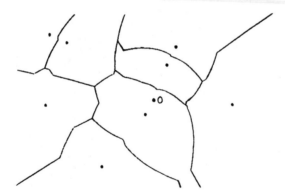

Figure 4.29: A d_M-Voronoi diagram.

In these investigations, d-straight arcs have proven a valuable substitute for straight lines; it was the d-star-shapedness of the Voronoi regions that implied the connectedness (d nice), and thus enabled the computation of the Voronoi diagram. The notion of *convexity* can also be generalized by means of d-straight arcs (cf. [53]): A set A is *(weakly) d-convex* iff it contains at least one d-straight arc from a to b, for any two points $a, b \in A$. Unfortunately, the Voronoi regions do not, in general, fulfill this property.

Remark 4.3.6 Let p and q be two points on the same radius, and assume that $|p| < |q|$ holds. Then $R(q,p)$ is not weakly d_M-convex.

In fact, there exists only one d_M-straight arc between the points v and w in $R(q,p)$, as depicted in Figure 4.28, and this arc is not fully contained in $R(q,p)$.

Concluding Remarks

In Chapters 2 and 3, we have generalized the concept of Voronoi diagrams to a situation where no distance measure is given, but a system of bisecting curves subject to certain combinatorial constraints. We have shown how to merge two abstract Voronoi diagrams, $V(L)$ and $V(R)$, where $L \cap R = \emptyset$, in a number of steps proportional to $|L \cup R|$, if the bisector of L and R contains no edge cycle (the algorithm can be run without this assumption, but then it will fail to compute the full bisector). On the one hand, our result clarifies which assumptions are really necessary in computing the Voronoi diagram by the divide-and-conquer method (convexity of the regions, for example, is superfluous; connectedness is sufficient). On the other hand, it provides us with a general tool: whenever a nice metric admits acyclic partitions of the set of sites, the Voronoi diagram can be computed within $O(n \log n)$ steps, relative to the complexity of the elementary bisector operations (Definition 3.4.3.1).

Criteria for a partition of the site set to be acyclic are given in Chapter 4. Both of them hold for all norms that have tractible bisectors (Definition 1.2.12, 4)), thereby generalizing previous work. Interesting metrics arise from regular city layouts. Whereas the Manhattan metric was the first non-Euclidean metric whose Voronoi diagrams were studied, our results also apply to the fan-shaped layout of Moscow. Here, a bisector consists of not more than 8 segments of hyperbolae (in polar coordinates), so the elementary operations can in fact be carried out in constant time. A more realistic model of Manhattan requires assigning different metrics (L_1 and L_2, for example) to different regions. We have a criterion for certain classes of such metrics to admit acyclic partitions, so that their Voronoi diagrams can also be computed by a divide-and-conquer technique.

A natural and important question is what can be done if acyclic partitions are not available, e.g., for point sites with additive weights. In the meantime, a first solution to this more general problem has been provided by Mehlhorn, Ó'Dúnlaing, and Meiser [43]. They showed how to compute an abstract Voronoi diagram of n sites in *expected* time $O(n \log n)$, using a randomized incremental construction introduced in [15]. Their algorithm rests on the analysis done in Chapter 2. It needs no assumptions about the existence of acyclic partitions. The first version, however, did only apply to curve systems in general position (only proper cross-points, not more than three curves at a point). Meanwhile, it was shown by Klein, Mehlhorn, and Meiser [36] how to generalize the incremental algorithm to admissible curve systems that are subject only to the following constraint: two p-bisectors must not touch at their p-sides. With this restriction, the Voronoi regions do not contain cut-points, i.e. their boundaries have no multiple points. On the other hand, this assumption is perhaps not too restrictive, in view of Lemma 4.2.2.

As for *abstract Voronoi diagrams*, the following major problems are still open. *Is there an $O(n \log n)$ worst case algorithm that runs without acylicity assumptions? Can the incremental construction be generalized to closed bisecting curves (as occuring in the Voronoi diagram on a cone, for example; see [17])? To higher dimensions? And finally, how can these techniques be implemented in order to obtain an efficient generic algorithm for the computation of all sorts of concrete Voronoi diagrams?* It was shown in [36] that it is sufficient to implement the computation of an abstract diagram of five sites. Using such a module, the abstract Voronoi diagram of an arbitrary number of sites can be constructed in a purely combinatorial way.

There also many interesting open questions concerning *concrete Voronoi diagrams*. To implement elementary bisector operations, *knowledge of the bisectors* is needed. An interesting question is on the complexity of the bisectors in a composite metric, if the number of regions to which different metrics are assigned, and their geometric complexity, are considered part of the problem size. Perhaps, an answer can be based on an *analysis of the straight arcs*, as in the case of the Moscow metric. The latter problem seems interesting in its own right, even if the constituent metrics are simple. Compositions of metrics $c \cdot L_2, c \in (0, \infty]$, have been investigated in [46] and [26].

Another natural question is what amount of *proximity information* on the points is comprised in a Voronoi diagram based on a non-Euclidean metric. It is not hard to see that, in a nice metric, the Voronoi region of a nearest neighbor, q, of p in S is neighboring the region of p (the closures of the regions may intersect in a point v only; but then all the regions represented at v belong to nearest neighbors of p, among them two that share an edge with $R(p, S)$). This fact can be proven analogously to Theorem 5.9 in [52]; only the straight line must be replaced with a d-straight arc. As in the Euclidean case (cf. Section 1.1), one obtains linear reductions of the proximity problems *closest pair* and *all nearest neighbors* to the construction of the Voronoi diagram. Essentially, the *nearest neighbor* problem in a nice metric can also be solved by means of the Voronoi diagram. The difficulty is that point location becomes much harder if the faces are bordered by curves. Preparata's *trapezoid method* for building up a location structure can be applied, if the curves are functions of a fixed coordinate (Remark 2, Chap. 2.3, [52]). However, locating a point needs the (possibly costly) elementary operation E1, as of Definition 3.4.3.1. Remark 4.3.6 indicates that one cannot hope for a generalization of those Voronoi properties that are related to convexity. An interesting problem is if a Delaunay triangulation exists in nice metrics (or in more restrictive classes), and what the connection with the Voronoi diagram is.

Finally, spaces other than the plane should be considered. *A curved surface in 3-space* can provide us with a much more realistic model of the earth, and it needs d-space, where $d > 3$, to attack problems from motion planning.

Bibliography

[1] S. Abramowski, B. Lang, and H. Müller. Moving regular k-gons in contact. In J. van Leeuwen, editor, *Graphtheoretic Concepts in Computer Science (WG '88)*, pages 229–242, Amsterdam. LNCS 344, Springer-Verlag, Berlin, 1989.

[2] A. V. Aho, J. E. Hopcroft, and J. D. Ullman. *The Design and Analysis of Computer Algorithms*. Addison-Wesley, Reading, Mass., 1974.

[3] B. Aronov. On the geodesic Voronoi diagram of point sites in a simple polygon. In *Proceedings 3rd ACM Symposium on Computational Geometry*, pages 39–49, Waterloo, 1987.

[4] P. F. Ash and E. D. Bolker. Generalized Dirichlet tesselations. *Geometriae Dedicata*, 20:209–243, 1986.

[5] P. F. Ash and E. D. Bolker. Recognizing Dirichlet tesselations. *Geometriae Dedicata*, 19:175–206, 1985.

[6] F. Aurenhammer. Power diagrams: Properties, algorithms and applications. *SIAM J. Comput.*, 16(1):78–96, 1987.

[7] F. Aurenhammer. *Voronoi Diagrams - A Survey*. Graz Technical University, 1988.

[8] M. Barner and F. Flohr. *Analysis II*. Walter de Gruyter, Berlin, 1983.

[9] J. Bentley. *Programming Pearls*. Addison-Wesley, Reading, Mass., 1986.

[10] B. Bollobás. *Extremal Graph Theory*. Academic Press, New York, 1978.

[11] K. Q. Brown. Voronoi diagrams from convex hulls. *Inf. Process. Lett.*, 9(5):223–228, 1979.

[12] A. Brüggemann-Klein and D. Wood. Drawing trees nicely with TeX. *Electronic Publishing, Origination, Dissemination, and Design*, to appear, 1989.

[13] H. Busemann. *The Geometry of Geodesics*. Academic Press, New York, 1955.

[14] L. P. Chew and R. L. Drysdale, III. Voronoi diagrams based on convex distance functions. In *Proceedings 1st ACM Symposium on Computational Geometry*, pages 235–244, Baltimore, 1985.

[15] K. L. Clarkson and P. W. Shor. Algorithms for diametral pairs and convex hulls that are optimal, randomized, and incremental. In *Proceedings 4th ACM Symposium on Computational Geometry*, pages 12–17, Urbana-Champaign, 1988.

[16] R. Cole. Reported by C. Ó'Dúnlaing, 1989.

[17] F. Dehne and R. Klein. A sweepcircle algorithm for Voronoi diagrams. In H. Göttler and H. J. Schneider, editors, *Graphtheoretic Concepts in Computer Science (WG '87)*, pages 59–70, Staffelstein. LNCS 314, Springer-Verlag, Berlin, 1988.

[18] B. Delaunay. Sur la sphère vide. *Bull. Acad. Sci. USSR, Classe Sci. Mat. Nat.*, 7:793–800, 1934.

[19] R. Descartes. *Principia Philosophiae*. Ludovicus Elzevirius, Amsterdam, 1644.

[20] Diercke. *Weltatlas*. Georg Westermann Verlag, Braunschweig, 1957.

[21] P. G. L. Dirichlet. Über die Reduction der positiven quadratischen Formen mit drei unbestimmten ganzen Zahlen. *J. Reine Angew. Math.*, 40:209–227, 1850.

[22] J. Dugundji. *Topology*. Allyn and Bacon, Boston, 1970.

[23] H. Edelsbrunner. *Algorithms in Combinatorial Geometry*. EATCS Monographs on Theoretical Computer Science, Volume 10, Springer-Verlag, Berlin, 1987.

[24] H. Edelsbrunner, J. O'Rourke, and R. Seidel. Constructing arrangements of lines and hyperplanes with applications. *SIAM J. Comput.*, 15:341–363, 1986.

[25] S. Fortune. A sweepline algorithm for Voronoi diagrams. *Algorithmica*, 2(2):153–174, 1987.

[26] L. Gewali, A. Meng, J. S. B. Mitchell, and S. Ntafos. Path planning in $0/1/\infty$ weighted regions with applications. In *Proceedings 4th ACM Symposium on Computational Geometry*, pages 266–278, Urbana-Champaign, 1988.

[27] A. Gibbons. *Algorithmic Graph Theory*. Cambridge University Press, Cambridge, 1985.

[28] H. Heusinger and H. Noltemeier. On separable and rectangular clusterings. In H. Noltemeier, editor, *Computational Geometry and its Applications (CG '88)*, pages 25–42, Würzburg. LNCS 333, Springer-Verlag, Berlin, 1988.

[29] S. J. Hong and F. P. Preparata. Convex hulls of finite sets of points in two and three dimensions. *Comm. ACM*, 20(2):87–93, 1977.

[30] F. K. Hwang. An $O(n \log n)$ algorithm for rectilinear minimal spanning trees. *J. ACM*, 26:177–182, 1979.

[31] D. G. Kirkpatrick. Optimal search in planar subdivisions. *SIAM J. Comput.*, 12(1):28–35, 1983.

[32] V. Klee. On the complexity of d-dimensional Voronoi diagrams. *Archiv der Mathematik*, 34:75–80, 1980.

[33] R. Klein. Abstract Voronoi diagrams and their applications (extended abstract). In H. Noltemeier, editor, *Computational Geometry and its Applications (CG '88)*, pages 148–157, Würzburg, 1988. LNCS 333, Springer-Verlag, Berlin, 1988.

[34] R. Klein. Voronoi diagrams in the Moscow metric (extended abstract). In J. van Leeuwen, editor, *Graphtheoretic Concepts in Computer Science (WG '88)*, pages 434–441, Amsterdam. LNCS 344, Springer-Verlag, Berlin, 1989.

[35] R. Klein. Combinatorial properties of abstract Voronoi diagrams. In M. Nagl, editor, *Graphtheoretic Concepts in Computer Science (WG '89)*, Rolduc, 1989. To appear in LNCS.

[36] R. Klein, K. Mehlhorn, and St. Meiser. Five sites are enough. Saarbrücken, 1989. Manuscript.

[37] R. Klein and D. Wood. Voronoi diagrams based on general metrics in the plane. In R. Cori and M. Wirsing, editors, *Proc. 5th Annual Symposium on Theoretical Aspects of Computer Science (STACS)*, pages 281–291, Bordeaux. LNCS 294, Springer-Verlag, Berlin, 1988.

[38] D. T Lee. Two-dimensional Voronoi diagrams in the L_p metric. *J. ACM*, 27:604–618, 1980.

[39] D. T. Lee and F. P. Preparata. Euclidean shortest paths in the presence of rectilinear barriers. *Networks*, 14(3):393–410, 1984.

[40] D. T. Lee and C. K. Wong. Voronoi diagrams in $L_1(L_\infty)$ metrics with 2-dimensional storage applications. *SIAM J. Comput.*, 9:200–211, 1980.

[41] D. Leven and M. Sharir. Planning a purely translational motion for a convex object in two-dimensional space using generalized Voronoi diagrams. *Discrete Comput. Geom.*, 2:9–31, 1987.

[42] K. Mehlhorn. *Data Structures and Algorithms 1: Sorting and Searching.* EATCS Monographs on Theoretical Computer Science, Volume 1, Springer-Verlag, Berlin, 1984.

[43] K. Mehlhorn, C. Ó'Dúnlaing, and St. Meiser. On the construction of abstract Voronoi diagrams. Presented at *Computational Geometry and its Applications (CG '89)*, Freiburg, 1989. Submitted for publication.

[44] St. Meiser. Oral communication, 1989.

[45] K. Menger. Untersuchungen über allgemeine Metrik, I, II, III. *Mathematische Annalen*, 100:75–163, 1928.

[46] J. S. B. Mitchell and Ch. H. Papadimitriou. The weighted region problem. In *Proceedings 3rd ACM Symposium on Computational Geometry*, pages 30–38, Waterloo, 1987.

[47] D. E. Muller and F. P. Preparata. Finding the intersection of two convex polyhedra. *Theoretical Computer Science*, 7(2):217–236, 1978.

[48] G. Nees. Regentengraphik und das ästhetische Laboratorium. Erlangen, 1988. Manuscript.

[49] M. H. A. Newman. *Elements of the Topology of Plane Sets of Points.* Cambridge University Press, Cambridge, 1951.

[50] O. Nurmi. *Algorithms for Computational Geometry.* PhD thesis, University of Karlsruhe, 1987.

[51] Th. Ottmann and P. Widmayer. Voronoi-Diagramme. Karlsruhe, 1986. Course notes on algorithms, programming techniques, and data structures.

[52] F. P. Preparata and M. I. Shamos. *Computational Geometry: An Introduction.* Springer-Verlag, New York, 1985.

[53] W. Rinow. *Die innere Geometrie der Metrischen Räume.* Grundlehren der Mathematischen Wissenschaften in Einzeldarstellungen, Volume 105, Springer-Verlag, Berlin, 1961.

[54] W. Rinow. *Topologie*. VEB Deutscher Verlag der Wissenschaften, Leipzig, 1975.

[55] S. Schuierer. *Der Radiosity Approach: Ein neuer Ansatz in der Realistischen Computergraphik*. Master's thesis, University of Karlsruhe, 1988.

[56] M. I. Shamos and D. Hoey. Closest-point problems. In *Proceedings 16th IEEE Symposium on Foundations of Computer Science*, pages 151–162, 1975.

[57] Y. A. Shreider. *What is distance?* Popular Lectures in Mathematics, The University of Chicago Press, Chicago, 1974.

[58] G. Voronoi. Nouvelles applications des paramètres continus à la théorie des formes quadratiques. Deuxième Mémoire: Recherches sur les parallélöedres primitifs. *J. Reine Angew. Math*, 134:198–287, 1908.

[59] G. Voronoi. Nouvelles applications des paramètres continus à la théorie des formes quadratiques. Premier Mémoire: Sur quelques propriétés des formes quadratiques positives parfaites. *J. Reine Angew. Math*, 133:97–178, 1907.

[60] P. Widmayer, Y. F. Wu, and C. K. Wong. Distance problems in computational geometry for fixed orientations. In *Proceedings 1st ACM Symposium on Computational Geometry*, pages 186–195, Baltimore, 1985.

[61] C. K. Yap. *An $O(n \log n)$ algorithm for the Voronoi diagram of a set of simple curve segments*. Technical Report 161, Computer Science Department, Courant Institute, New York University, 1985.

Vol. 352: J. Díaz, F. Orejas (Eds.), TAPSOFT '89. Volume 2. Proceedings, 1989. X, 389 pages. 1989.

Vol. 353: S. Hölldobler, Foundations of Equational Logic Programming. X, 250 pages. 1989. (Subseries LNAI).

Vol. 354: J.W. de Bakker, W.-P. de Roever, G. Rozenberg (Eds.), Linear Time, Branching Time and Partial Order in Logics and Models for Concurrency. VIII, 713 pages. 1989.

Vol. 355: N. Dershowitz (Ed.), Rewriting Techniques and Applications. Proceedings, 1989. VII, 579 pages. 1989.

Vol. 356: L. Huguet, A. Poli (Eds.), Applied Algebra, Algebraic Algorithms and Error-Correcting Codes. Proceedings, 1987. VI, 417 pages. 1989.

Vol. 357: T. Mora (Ed.), Applied Algebra, Algebraic Algorithms and Error-Correcting Codes. Proceedings, 1988. IX, 481 pages. 1989.

Vol. 358: P. Gianni (Ed.), Symbolic and Algebraic Computation. Proceedings, 1988. XI, 545 pages. 1989.

Vol. 359: D. Gawlick, M. Haynie, A. Reuter (Eds.), High Performance Transaction Systems. Proceedings, 1987. XII, 329 pages. 1989.

Vol. 360: H. Maurer (Ed.), Computer Assisted Learning – ICCAL '89. Proceedings, 1989. VII, 642 pages. 1989.

Vol. 361: S. Abiteboul, P.C. Fischer, H.-J. Schek (Eds.), Nested Relations and Complex Objects in Databases. VI, 323 pages. 1989.

Vol. 362: B. Lisper, Synthesizing Synchronous Systems by Static Scheduling in Space-Time. VI, 263 pages. 1989.

Vol. 363: A.R. Meyer, M.A. Taitslin (Eds.), Logic at Botik '89. Proceedings, 1989. X, 289 pages. 1989.

Vol. 364: J. Demetrovics, B. Thalheim (Eds.), MFDBS 89. Proceedings, 1989. VI, 428 pages. 1989.

Vol. 365: E. Odijk, M. Rem, J.-C. Syre (Eds.), PARLE '89. Parallel Architectures and Languages Europe. Volume I. Proceedings, 1989. XIII, 478 pages. 1989.

Vol. 366: E. Odijk, M. Rem, J.-C. Syre (Eds.), PARLE '89. Parallel Architectures and Languages Europe. Volume II. Proceedings, 1989. XIII, 442 pages. 1989.

Vol. 367: W. Litwin, H.-J. Schek (Eds.), Foundations of Data Organization and Algorithms. Proceedings, 1989. VIII, 531 pages. 1989.

Vol. 368: H. Boral, P. Faudemay (Eds.), IWDM '89, Database Machines. Proceedings, 1989. VI, 387 pages. 1989.

Vol. 369: D. Taubner, Finite Representations of CCS and TCSP Programs by Automata and Petri Nets. X. 168 pages. 1989.

Vol. 370: Ch. Meinel, Modified Branching Programs and Their Computational Power. VI, 132 pages. 1989.

Vol. 371: D. Hammer (Ed.), Compiler Compilers and High Speed Compilation. Proceedings, 1988. VI. 242 pages. 1989.

Vol. 372: G. Ausiello, M. Dezani-Ciancaglini, S. Ronchi Della Rocca (Eds.), Automata, Languages and Programming. Proceedings, 1989. XI, 788 pages. 1989.

Vol. 373: T. Theoharis, Algorithms for Parallel Polygon Rendering. VIII, 147 pages. 1989.

Vol. 374: K.A. Robbins, S. Robbins, The Cray X-MP/Model 24. VI, 165 pages. 1989.

Vol. 375: J.L.A. van de Snepscheut (Ed.), Mathematics of Program Construction. Proceedings, 1989. VI, 421 pages. 1989.

Vol. 376: N.E. Gibbs (Ed.), Software Engineering Education. Proceedings, 1989. VII, 312 pages. 1989.

Vol. 377: M. Gross, D. Perrin (Eds.), Electronic Dictionaries and Automata in Computational Linguistics. Proceedings, 1987. V, 110 pages. 1989.

Vol. 378: J.H. Davenport (Ed.), EUROCAL '87. Proceedings, 1987. VIII, 499 pages. 1989.

Vol. 379: A. Kreczmar, G. Mirkowska (Eds.), Mathematical Foundations of Computer Science 1989. Proceedings, 1989. VIII, 605 pages. 1989.

Vol. 380: J. Csirik, J. Demetrovics, F. Gécseg (Eds.), Fundamentals of Computation Theory. Proceedings, 1989. XI, 493 pages. 1989.

Vol. 381: J. Dassow, J. Kelemen (Eds.), Machines, Languages, and Complexity. Proceedings, 1988. VI, 244 pages. 1989.

Vol. 382: F. Dehne, J.-R. Sack, N. Santoro (Eds.), Algorithms and Data Structures. WADS '89. Proceedings, 1989. IX, 592 pages. 1989.

Vol. 383: K. Furukawa, H. Tanaka, T. Fujisaki (Eds.), Logic Programming '88. Proceedings, 1988. VII, 251 pages. 1989 (Subseries LNAI).

Vol. 384: G.A. van Zee, J.G.G. van de Vorst (Eds.), Parallel Computing 1988. Proceedings, 1988. V, 135 pages. 1989.

Vol. 385: E. Börger. H. Kleine Büning, M.M. Richter (Eds.), CSL '88. Proceedings, 1988. VI, 399 pages. 1989.

Vol. 386: J.E. Pin (Ed.), Formal Properties of Finite Automata and Applications. Proceedings, 1988. VIII, 260 pages. 1989.

Vol. 387: C. Ghezzi, J.A. McDermid (Eds.), ESEC '89. 2nd European Software Engineering Conference. Proceedings, 1989. VI, 496 pages. 1989.

Vol. 388: G. Cohen, J. Wolfmann (Eds.), Coding Theory and Applications. Proceedings, 1988. IX, 329 pages. 1989.

Vol. 389: D.H. Pitt, D.E. Rydeheard, P. Dybjer, A.M. Pitts, A. Poigné (Eds.), Category Theory and Computer Science. Proceedings, 1989. VI, 365 pages. 1989.

Vol. 390: J.P. Martins, E.M. Morgado (Eds.), EPIA 89. Proceedings, 1989. XII, 400 pages. 1989 (Subseries LNAI).

Vol. 391: J.-D. Boissonnat, J.-P. Laumond (Eds.), Geometry and Robotics. Proceedings, 1988. VI, 413 pages. 1989.

Vol. 392: J.-C. Bermond, M. Raynal (Eds.), Distributed Algorithms. Proceedings, 1989. VI, 315 pages. 1989.

Vol. 393: H. Ehrig, H. Herrlich, H.-J. Kreowski, G. Preuß (Eds.), Categorical Methods in Computer Science. VI, 350 pages. 1989.

Vol. 394: M. Wirsing, J.A. Bergstra (Eds.), Algebraic Methods: Theory, Tools and Applications. VI, 558 pages. 1989.

Vol. 395: M. Schmidt-Schauß, Computational Aspects of an Order-Sorted Logic with Term Declarations. VIII, 171 pages. 1989. (Subseries LNAI).

Vol. 396: T.A. Berson, T. Beth (Eds.), Local Area Network Security. Proceedings, 1989. IX, 152 pages. 1989.

Vol. 397: K.P. Jantke (Ed.), Analogical and Inductive Inference. IX, 338 pages. 1989. (Subseries LNAI).

Vol. 398: B. Banieqbal, H. Barringer, A. Pnueli (Eds.), Temporal Logic in Specification. Proceedings, 1987. VI, 448 pages. 1989.

Vol. 399: V. Cantoni, R. Creutzburg, S. Levialdi, G. Wolf (Eds.), Recent Issues in Pattern Analysis and Recognition. VII, 400 pages. 1989.

Vol. 400: R. Klein, Concrete and Abstract Voronoi Diagrams. IV, 167 pages. 1989.